The Country Habit
An Anthology

The Country Habit
An Anthology

Edited and Introduced by

Joanna Trollope

BANTAM PRESS

LONDON · NEW YORK · TORONTO · SYDNEY · AUCKLAND

TRANSWORLD PUBLISHERS LTD
61–63 Uxbridge Road, London W5 5SA

TRANSWORLD PUBLISHERS (AUSTRALIA) PTY LTD
15–25 Helles Avenue, Moorebank, NSW 2170

TRANSWORLD PUBLISHERS (NZ) LTD
3 William Pickering Drive, Albany, Auckland

Published 1993 by Bantam Press
a division of Transworld Publishers Ltd
Copyright © compilation and Introduction Joanna Trollope 1993

A catalogue record for this book is available from the British Library.
ISBN 0593 02690X

Typeset in 11/14 New Baskerville by
Chippendale Type Ltd, Otley, West Yorkshire
Printed in Great Britain by
Bath Press Colourbooks

For My Mother

CONTENTS

INTRODUCTION

THERE IS SOMETHING SINGULAR IN THE WAY THE ENGLISH feel about the countryside and country life. It's true that they share with other northern races a romantic passion for the Anglo-Saxon rural idyll, that innocent paradise portrayed by the Swedish artist, Carl Larsson, in his paintings of sturdy little kerchiefed girls herding geese through orchards, or white muslin curtains blowing out of open windows between pots of robust geraniums, but they also feel something above and beyond that. They seem to possess an instinct for the country, an instinct which has led, at a practical level, to that admired and much imitated social unit, the English village, and at a more mystical level, to an almost pantheistic appreciation of landscape. A lot of English people may not want to live in the country, but they wish, even need, to visit it regularly, and would know themselves doomed if, by some awful accident, it suddenly wasn't there any more.

Historically, of course, as Mark Girouard has pointed out in the introduction to his splendid *Life in the English Country House*, the great empty spaces of rural England spelled power rather than our modern and feebler notion of a refuge from urban stress. The power of owning land lay, for centuries, not in the simple possession of acres, but in the tenants who leased them from a landowner, and the rents they paid. Owning enough land, and subsequently laying claim to the attendant tenant followers who lived on it, made an ambitious man likely to catch the eye of the Government in the matter of advancement. A good government job then brought in the money with which to buy more land, and, with it, more support both from increased numbers of tenants and from fellow landowners anxious to be associated with a rising man. It was a system pragmatic to the point of cynicism, a world away from any later and less steely notion that to live in the country was to stand at least a reasonable chance of finding both oneself and an inner peace. It was also a system that lasted, in the sense that England's wealth and power remained country- rather than town-based until the last century, and even when the economic balance did swing in favour of cities, the first thing that the newly rich did – and still do – was to buy themselves a country estate. Even today, it looks more significant, and enviable, to possess a baroque house sitting in its own portion of Wiltshire, or Yorkshire, than to own even the grandest of town houses.

Yet it's worth noticing that these great landowners, past and present, have seldom farmed, and if they have, almost never at a profit. This gives us some idea of how the countryside must have looked in the past, and how wild it must have been, apart from patches of parkland, compared with the agricultural domesticity that has tidied up so much of the landscape that we know as 'countryside' today. It also gives us, even more importantly, an idea of how profoundly unsentimental our ancestors were about the great wastes of rough land across which they had to struggle to achieve the basic business of life and livelihood. We are now, by contrast, inclined to be woefully — and mistakenly — sentimental about country life, but it's salutary to remember that for all but a very lucky few, living out in the sticks has only been even tolerable, from a practical point of view, for under fifty years. Before that, in most English villages, and certainly out in the wilds, there was no piped water, no electricity or gas, and definitely no mains drainage. A friend of mine growing up in a Rutlandshire village in the early fifties, clearly remembers the nightsoil cart trundling round the cottages each morning, and that is only forty years ago.

Even now, country life is not for the faint-hearted. There is more weather in the country, more inconvenience, more dullness, less culture, less society, more prurience, more mud. Mud, for newcomers to country life, often proves to be their Waterloo. Yet for all the drawbacks, and despite the tough and uncompromising history of English rural life, the English continue to feel, with a determination that would be obstinacy if it were not fired by some powerful instinct of both union with and salvation in the countryside, that that is where they belong, and, more often than not, in a community like this:

> A tall old church on a hillside, a pub selling the local brew, a pretty stream, a football pitch, a handsome square vicarage with a cedar of Lebanon shading it, a school with jars of tadpoles in the window, three shops with doorbells,

a Tudor mansion, half a dozen farms and a lot of quaint
cottages.

Such a place, said Ronald Blythe who wrote that passage in
Akenfield, typifies 'our national village cult', that beloved myth
that suggests that somewhere out there among the fields and
woods there still survives a timeless natural existence of innocence and incorruption. It's nothing new, this yearning for an
earthly Elysium – the painters and craftsmen of the pre-
Raphaelite movement, men such as William Morris, felt it after
all, at just such a time of rampant materialism at the end of
their century as we feel so painfully at the end of ours – and it is
more than understandable even for reasons that are less
exalted than the longing for a return to purity and first
principles. One of those reasons, as far as landscape and
architecture is concerned, is the sheer look of the thing.

The aesthetic roll-call of beautiful bits of English landscape is
legendary. To name but a few, the Lake District, the Kentish
Weald, the Yorkshire Dales, the Cotswold hills, the salt marshes
of the east coast and the cliffs and river estuaries of the west,
the Sussex Downs, the northern moors are all not just lovely –
sometimes breathtakingly so – in themselves, but wonderfully
various. And then there are English villages. Try as they might
the world over, with the ingenious use of clapboard or stilts or
horsehair tents, no-one else can hold a candle to the visual
impact of an English village. The combination of local materials
– stone, brick, thatch, flints, timber, slate – and the English gift
for vernacular domestic architecture has created settlements
that are entirely satisfying to look at. They have charm, oddity,
elegance and harmony, and they also look as if they had grown
out of the landscape instead of being merely parked upon it.

This beauty is also, most seductively, more than skin deep.
You can almost always, if you think about it, imagine yourself
living in an English village house. They look, and usually are,
easy to live in because that is what they were designed for,
rather than primarily for fashion or expediency. English rectories and cottages and manor houses have a humanity about
them almost no-one can resist; they feel welcoming and familiar,

they don't threaten or overwhelm. Who could blame anyone living in a city flat three floors up above traffic lights and an all-night takeaway, for persuading themselves that the solution to all their problems lies in being instead in an old beamed room with a ticking clock and a cat and a view of cow-parsley and a medieval church tower?

Who indeed can blame anyone for looking for a lost Eden? Man has been on the hunt for it ever since he lost it, after all, and the fact that the Edens of this world are fast disappearing only makes them the more precious. The apprehension that this is so, and that this vital, mysterious rural commodity is frighteningly fragile, makes many newcomers to villages extremely thin-skinned about the reality of country life. They arrive, most understandably, complete with their dreams and prejudices, and then they are inevitably deeply upset by an actuality that doesn't match.

The trouble is fundamentally not just one of shock at the harshness of nature – there's precious little sentiment in the way, for example, that a stoat kills a kingfisher – but more importantly that the dream of country life isn't just one of physical natural beauty, but of human beauty too. People in villages, says the rural myth, are kinder, simpler, more honest. People in villages, says reality, are no different from people anywhere else; the difference exists only in the visibility of behaviour in smaller populations. Kindness and human warmth certainly stand out, but so do cruelty and greed. Loneliness and privacy are equally impossible; a benevolent interest in your welfare is matched by a salacious interest in your activities.

The notion of simple people living in simple communities depends, of course, upon that great traditional industry of the countryside, namely agriculture. There is an assumption that working on the land and with animals – i.e. close to nature – has an almost uplifting and certainly morally improving effect. But is this assumption as much a myth as the rural dream? I saw, not long ago, a northern hill farmer on Channel Four's *Famous for Four Minutes* who, when asked about the satisfactions of his life, snorted and said bluntly, 'You have to be right daft to do

this.' It's an age-old observation. Mark Girouard quotes Sir Henry Unton, wailing from the country in the 1590s that 'my clownish life doth deprive me of all intelligence and comfort', and his was only one voice from the past complaining bitterly of dirt, boredom and the sense of helpless imprisonment by rural isolation.

Sower at work, from the Luttrell *Psalter, fourteenth century*

Yet, tenaciously, still they come, from daily walkers and fishermen through weekend-only cottage owners to those boldly exchanging one way of life for quite another. The very tenacity seems to point to something deeper than just a stubborn romantic hope, and that something appears to be this specifically English feeling about landscape and the life that is lived in it, a feeling that the English themselves are hardly aware of and almost never articulate, except when it is done for them by a composer such as Elgar or a poet such as Wordsworth. When it *is* articulated in this way, they respond with fervour, and it's hardly an exaggeration to call this profound and passionate attitude pantheism.

The Romantic poets, notably Coleridge and Wordsworth, were in no doubt about identifying the natural universe with some kind of spiritual being or force which was not, in their case, the orthodox God of Christianity. For them, everything in the world, even inert objects like rocks and stones, was both alive and interrelated and therefore possessed:

> A virtue which irradiates and exalts
> All objects through all intercourse of self.

Thus it was natural and logical for them to choose country life and characters as subjects for their *Lyrical Ballads*, as they explained in the preface:

> Low and rustic life was generally chosen because in that situation the essential passions of the heart find a better soil in which they can attain their maturity, are less under restraint and speak a plainer and more emphatic language; because in that situation our elementary feelings exist in a state of greater simplicity and consequently may be more accurately contemplated and more forcibly communicated; because the manners of rural life germinate from those elementary feelings; and from the necessary character of rural occupations are more easily comprehended; and are more durable; and lastly because in that situation the passions of men are incorporated with the beautiful and permanent forms of nature.

It is that last statement that the English seem to believe, almost unconsciously, with all their hearts. Nature is so ancient and so lovely that it appears to be a visible expression of all those spiritual concepts which we have words for but no precise imaginative grasp of – infinity, eternity, the soul, the spirit. Why this ability to feel a profound sense of unearthly (as well as earthly) belonging in the countryside should be so English is as mysterious as the feeling itself, but English it certainly is, sweeping not just through the music of Vaughan Williams and Elgar, and the novels of Thomas Hardy, and the poetry of George Herbert and John Clare and Gerard Manley Hopkins, but even through reluctant old crosspatches like Thomas Carlyle, who tried, in vain, to deny that nature meant a thing to him. In November 1872, the poet William Allingham suggested to Carlyle that 'Nature might be a powerful help to religious feeling' and subsequently recorded the great man's reply in his journal:

> C. (as I knew he would) – Ho! there's not much in that. A great deal of sham and affectation is in the raptures people express about Nature; ecstasies over mountains and water-fall etc. I perceive that most people really get much the same amount of good out of all that as I do myself: I have a kind of content in it; but any kind of Nature does well enough. I used to find the moorlands answer my purpose as well as anything – great, brown, shaggy expanses, here and there a huge boulder stone – 'There you lie, God knows how long!'

How long indeed and how long can it all last? The traditional and vital bond between the English and their lovely land depends not just upon being able to tramp the moors and fish the rivers and walk through the woods and gaze across the valleys, but being able, practically, to live among them too. A living landscape may be made up, in Wordsworthian terms, of rocks and stones, but it must be made up of people too, and it's hard to keep people on the land in the 1990s with the sharp decline in farming.

Farming in England has in fact been on the decline since the 1860s but the rate of its failure has accelerated wildly in the last decade. Judging by appearances, such a state of affairs seems impossible. One looks about at our well-husbanded countryside full of weed-free crops and stout beasts and one thinks: how on earth can all this prosperity spell *failure*? Yet it does. It spells failure precisely because, unlike the farmers of the past, the farmers of the present have farmed too well. Before the Second World War, we only produced 30 per cent of the food we needed because we could get cheap food from the Empire. After the war, and long before the advent of the EEC in 1973, there was a concerted European effort to grow more food as a direct reaction to the hunger of the war years and a general determination that Europe should never go hungry again. The

Common Agricultural Policy, born to achieve this, has simply worked far too well and hasn't managed to adapt to its own success, with the result that we all know so well – Europe has whole mountains and lakes of surplus food, and the value of it all has inevitably, and drastically, dropped.

The subsequent change, for life in the modern countryside, is dramatic. No longer can rural England see itself as a jealously guarded agricultural workshop, and those sweet birthday-card visions of spring sowing and lambing time and harvest homes may well become as much images of a vanished past as milkmaids with their pails and smockfrocked shepherds with their crooks, standing in patient hopefulness at a long-ago Wessex hiring fair. Indeed, something much more sad, and savage, has taken the place of our cherished Constable vision of a gently, happily busy agricultural land. We have now a bleak

Children watching threshing at Westerham, Kent, 1939

picture of increasing rural homelessness – at a higher rate than urban homelessness – decaying villages, and ruined farmers committing suicide in the quiet despair peculiar to country people. These tragedies seem able to attract no official attention; in 1992 the budget for the national Rural Development Commission was only 4 million pounds, while the city of Bootle alone received 37.5 million pounds to fight its inner-city problems. Even at its most optimistic, the language of the modern countryside no longer speaks in terms of growth and good harvests, but is instead now full of words like 'environmental' and 'diversification' as farmers try and find non-agricultural ways to earn a living, and rural communities try and adapt to increasing numbers of newcomers who may not wish to take everything as they find it, but who do, unquestionably, create both jobs and custom across scattered groups of country people cruelly short of both.

And so it will go on. The economics of the turn-of-the-century countryside will shift and modify, as farms give way to nature parks and golf courses and sites for rural industries, and the rural population will shift and modify along with the economics as it has always done. Yet powerful though these forces are, and radical as the changes that they bring with them are, they will not alter the fundamental English feeling that it is their inalienable right and innate place to live in, or within reach of, that countryside where light and dark and sun and rain dictate a natural rhythm of life that no scientific sophistication can really alter. We may no longer be able to live precisely as Laurie Lee did in the twenties, in a community where 'the year revolved around the village, the festivals around the year, the Church around the festivals, the Squire around the Church and the village around the Squire', but we can still live, without great difficulty, in a similar spirit. The English, however they earn their bread, will keep living country life because, quite simply, they need to. Even in the depths of the economic recession of the nineties, it has been startling and wonderful to notice, from estate agents' windows, that the price of land hasn't dropped anything like as far, or as fast, as the price of houses.

GOD IS GLORIFIED IN THE SUN AND MOON, IN THE rare fabrick of the honeycomb, in the discipline of the Bees, in the œconomy of the Pismires, in the little houses of birds, in the curiosity of an eye, God being pleased to delight in those little images and reflexes of himself from those pretty mirrours, which like a crevice in a wall thorow a narrow perspective transmit the species of a vast excellency.

BISHOP JEREMY TAYLOR

SPRING

MY DEAR WILLIAM,

Our severest winter, commonly called the spring, is now over, and I find myself seated in my favourite recess, the greenhouse. In such a situation, so silent, so shady, where no human foot is heard, and where only my myrtles presume to peep in at the window, you may suppose I have no interruption to complain of, and that my thoughts are perfectly at my command.

But the beauties of the spot are themselves an interruption; my attention is called upon by those very myrtles, by a double row of grass pinks just beginning to blossom, and by a bed of beans already in bloom; and you are to consider it, if you please, as no small proof of my regard that though you have so many powerful rivals, I disengage myself from them all, and devote this hour entirely to you . . .

WILLIAM COWPER, *letter to William Unwin*

SPRING

Nothing is so beautiful as Spring—
    When weeds, in wheels, shoot long and lovely and lush;
    Thrush's eggs look little low heavens, and thrush
Through the echoing timber does so rinse and wring
The ear, it strikes like lightnings to hear him sing;
    The glassy peartree leaves and blooms, they brush
    The descending blue; that blue is all in a rush
With richness; the racing lambs too have fair their fling.

What is all this juice and all this joy?
    A strain of the earth's sweet being in the beginning
In Eden garden.— Have, get, before it cloy,

Before it cloud, Christ, lord, and sour with sinning,
Innocent mind and Mayday in girl and boy,
Most, O maid's child, thy choice and worthy the winning.

GERARD MANLEY HOPKINS

TO MAKE ORINGE MARMALAD,

TAKE YO\` ORINGE RINDES PARE THEM AND BOYLE THEM UNTILL they bee very softe, then take them out of the water and bray them very smale in a morter, then take faire water some suger & the Juice of 3. or 4. oringes boyle and scum yt, then put in yo\` oringe stuffe, let yt boyle a quarter of an hower them poure yt out and let yt stand, to a pound of oringes you must take a pound of pipines pared and cored and to every pound of pipines a pound of suger & a pinte of water, let the water and suger boyle and bee scumed and then put in yo\` pipines and boyle them till they are very tender then breake them to peeces and put yo\` oringe stuffe to them, let them boyle together still stiringe of yt until yt will cut

LADY ELINOR FETTIPLACE, *1604*

AFTER THE KINGS HAD GONE WITH THE VARIOUS SUNDAYS after Epiphany – we never relished 'Sundays after' – we began to think of the first primroses. Early snowdrops in Joe Nott's orchard at Trevarrick were winter-white and cold, almost unearthly. Lambstails and daisies, celandines and colts-foot would appear. Then someone would find the first wild primrose. We did not count garden primroses as genuine 'firsts'. Often the first would be discovered at Pitts, the cliffs beyond Perhaver; or in Coosy Lane by Rescassa; or at Putt, between Trevarrick and Trevennen wood; or at Sentries, the

OPPOSITE: *The Double-Wheeled Plough from* Newe Tract for Husbandmen *by John Fitzherbert, 1523*

25

steep fields behind Cotna, or in Polsue Lane; or by Galowras Mill, about midway between Cotna and Mevagissey. After the first primrose had been found it was surprising how the families of buds grew, and soon someone would bring in a tiny

bunch for my mother to wear; then in the twinkling of an eye we would be 'going to pick primroses'. We took a basket and a little wool to tie up the bunches, and fairy-cakes to eat. These little cakes made of flour, ground rice, sugar, milk and eggs

Bringing Home the May *by H.P. Robinson, 1862*

27

were as sacred to primrosing as apple pasties were to sunshine holidays on Hemmick beach. We would set out soon after midday dinner. Often it would be cold in the early spring, and we would walk far to gather very few flowers. We spotted the buds and remembered to look for them the next week. We picked half-opened darlings, and put in plenty of crinkled leaves to swell our bunches, and feathers of moss for a fairy edging. But when all the hosts of the primroses were out we hardly knew which to pick. I used to whisper to the glorious ones we missed that it was not that they weren't beautiful. I had some vague idea that their feelings were hurt if they were left. Cap'n said this was very silly; that any primrose would rather stay in the hedge or wood. But Susan and I did not think so. We imagined that the other primroses in the family (belonging to one particular root) would think the chosen one exalted. We used to imagine the other primroses telling the buds what happened to some of their relations. Sometimes we put wild violets with our primrose bunches. At one place in Trevennen woods white wild violets grew, scented, and greatly prized. We hunted for the unusual and rare; double primroses, and red ones coloured like polyanthus, and branching primroses growing cowslip-wise from a thick central stalk. Now I think single flowers lovelier than double; they are more clear and delicate in shape. But I can still see in my mind's eye a wonderful double primrose my father once found. And the richly glowing double daffodils (we called them Lent lilies) which grew in orchards and in the steep field below Caerhays Rectory have to me the very essence and virtue of those who come before the swallow dares. The little single Lent lilies which grew in Trevennen wood did not dance; often they shivered. The double ones had dancing hearts.

ANNE TRENEER, *from* School House in the Wind

SONG IMITATED FROM THE ITALIAN

Oh shadie vales, O faire inriched meades
O sacred woods, sweete fields, and rising mountaines,
O painted flowers, greene herbes, where Flora treads
Refreshed by wanton windes and wartrie fountaines.

O all you winged queristers of woode
That pierced aloft your former paines report
And strait againe recount with pleasant mood
Your present joyes in sweete and seemly sort.

O all you creatures, whosoever thrive
On mother earth, in seas, by aire or fire,
More blest are you than I here under sunne:
Love dies in me, whenas he does revive
In you; I perish under beauties ire
Where after stormes, windes, frost, your life is wonne.

THOMAS LODGE

IF I SHOULD EVER BY CHANCE

If I should ever by chance grow rich
I'll buy Codham, Cockridden, and Childerditch,
Roses, Pyrgo, and Lapwater,
And let them all to my elder daughter.
The rent I shall ask of her will be only
Each year's first violets, white and lonely,
The first primroses and orchises—
She must find them before I do, that is.
But if she finds a blossom on furze
Without rent they shall all for ever be hers,
Codham, Cockridden, and Childerditch,
Roses, Pyrgo, and Lapwater—
I shall give them all to my elder daughter.

EDWARD THOMAS

THE QUESTION

I dreamed that, as I wandered by the way,
   Bare Winter suddenly was changed to Spring,
And gentle odours led my steps astray,
   Mixed with a sound of waters murmuring
Along a shelving bank of turf, which lay
   Under a copse, and hardly dared to fling
Its green arms round the bosom of the stream,
But kissed it and then fled, as thou mightest in dream.

There grew pied wind-flowers and violets,
   Daisies, those pearled Arcturi of the earth,
The constellated flower that never sets;
   Faint oxlips; tender blue-bells, at whose birth
The sod scarce heaved; and that tall flower that wets—
   Like a child, half in tenderness and mirth—
Its mother's face with Heaven's collected tears,
When the low wind, its playmate's voice, it hears.

And in the warm hedge grew lush eglantine,
   Green cowbind and the moonlight-coloured may
And cherry-blossoms, and white cups, whose wine
   Was the bright dew, yet drained not by the day;
And wild rose, and ivy serpentine
   With its dark buds and leaves, wandering astray;
And flowers azure, black, and streaked with gold,
Fairer than any wakened eyes behold.

And nearer to the river's trembling edge
   There grew broad flag-flowers, purple prankt with white,
And starry river-buds among the sedge,
   And floating water-lilies, broad and bright,
Which lit the oak that overhung the hedge
   With moonlight beams of their own watery light;
And bulrushes, and reeds of such deep green
As soothed the dazzled eye with sober sheen.

Methought that of these visionary flowers
    I made a nosegay, bound in such a way
That the same hues, which in their natural bowers
    Were mingled or opposed, the like array
Kept these imprisoned children of the Hours
    Within my hand – and then, elate and gay,
I hastened to the spot whence I had come,
That I might there present it! – Oh! to whom?

PERCY BYSSHE SHELLEY

SPRING

Spring, the sweet Spring, is the year's pleasant king;
Then blooms each thing, then maids dance in a ring,
Cold doth not sting, the pretty birds do sing,
    Cuckoo, jug-jug, pu-we, to-witta-woo!

The palm and may make country houses gay,
Lambs frisk and play, the shepherds pipe all day,
And we hear aye birds tune this merry lay,
    Cuckoo, jug-jug, pu-we, to-witta-woo!

The fields breathe sweet, the daisies kiss our feet,
Young lovers meet, old wives a-sunning sit,
In every street these tunes our ears do greet,
    Cuckoo, jug-jug, pu-we, to-witta-woo!
      Spring! the sweet Spring!

THOMAS NASH

NATURE

PSALM 65

9 Thou visitest the earth, and blessest it: thou makest it very plenteous.

10 The river of God is full of water: thou preparest their corn, for so thou providest for the earth.

11 Thou waterest her furrows, thou sendest rain into the little valleys thereof: thou makest it soft with the drops of rain, and blessest the increase of it.

12 Thou crownest the year with thy goodness: and thy clouds drop fatness.

13 They shall drop upon the dwellings of the wilderness: and the little hills shall rejoice on every side.

14 The folds shall be full of sheep: the valleys also shall stand so thick with corn, that they shall laugh and sing.

LOVE OF NATURE

THE LOVE OF NATURE IS EVER RETURNED DOUBLE TO US, not only the delighter in our delight, but by linking our sweetest, but of themselves perishable feelings to distinct and vivid images, which we ourselves, at times, and which a thousand casual recollections, recall to our memory. She is the preserver, the treasurer of our joys. Even in sickness and nervous diseases, she has peopled our imagination with lovely forms which have sometimes overpowered the inward pain and brought with them their old sensations. And even when all men have seemed to desert us and the friend of our heart has passed on, with one glance from his 'cold disliking eye'— yet even then the blue heaven is spread out and bends over us, and the little tree still shelters us under its plumage as a second cope, a domestic firmament, and the low creeping gale will sigh in the heath-plant and soothe us by sound of sympathy till the lulled grief loses itself in fixed gaze on the purple heath-blossom, till the present beauty becomes a vision of memory.

SAMUEL TAYLOR COLERIDGE, *from* Anima Poetae

THE POPLAR FIELD

The poplars are fell'd, farewell to the shade
And the whispering sound of the cool colonnade:
The winds play no longer and sing in the leaves,
Nor Ouse on his bosom their image receives.

Twelve years have elapsed since I first took a view
Of my favourite field, and the bank where they grew:
And now in the grass behold they are laid,
And the tree is my seat that once lent me a shade.

The blackbird has fled to another retreat
Where the hazels afford him a screen from the heat;
And the scene where his melody charm'd me before
Resounds with his sweet-flowing ditty no more.

My fugitive years are all hasting away,
And I must ere long lie as lowly as they,
With a turf on my breast and a stone at my head,
Ere another such grove shall arise in its stead.

'Tis a sight to engage me, if anything can,
To muse on the perishing pleasures of man;
Short-lived as we are, our enjoyments, I see,
Have a still shorter date, and die sooner than we.

WILLIAM COWPER

WILTSHIRE DOWNS

The cuckoo's double note
Loosened like bubbles from a drowning throat
Floats through the air
In mockery of pipit, lark and stare.

The stable-boys thud by
Their horses slinging divots at the sky
And with bright hooves
Printing the sodden turf with lucky grooves.

As still as a windhover
A shepherd in his flapping coat leans over
His tall sheep-crook
And shearlings, tegs and yoes cons like a book.

And one tree-crowned long barrow
Stretched like a sow that has brought forth her farrow
Hides a king's bones
Lying like broken sticks among the stones.

ANDREW YOUNG

THE SUSSEX DOWNS

THOUGH I HAVE NOW TRAVELLED THE *SUSSEX-DOWNS* upwards of thirty years, yet I still investigate that chain of majestic mountains with fresh admiration year by year; and I think I see new beauties every time I traverse it. The range, which runs from *Chichester* eastward as far as *East-Bourn*, is about sixty miles in length, and is called *The South Downs*, properly speaking, only round *Lewes*. As you pass along, you command a noble view of the wild, or weald, on one hand, and the broad downs and sea on the other. Mr. *Ray* used to visit a family just at the foot of these hills, and was so ravished with the prospect from *Plumptonplain*, near *Lewes*, that he mentions those scapes in his 'Wisdom of God in the Works of the Creation,' with the utmost satisfaction, and thinks them equal to any thing he had seen in the finest parts of Europe.

For my own part, I think there is somewhat peculiarly sweet and amusing in the shapely figured aspect of chalk-hills, in preference to those of stone, which are rugged, broken, abrupt, and shapeless.

Perhaps I may be singular in my opinion, and not so happy as to convey to you the same idea, but I never contemplate these mountains without thinking I perceive somewhat analogous to growth in their gentle swellings and smooth fungus-like protuberances, their fluted sides, and regular hollows and slopes, that carry at once the air of vegetative dilatation and expansion . . . Or was there ever a time when these immense masses of calcareous matter were thrown into fermentation by some adventitious moisture,—were raised and leavened into such shapes by some plastic power, and so made to swell and heave their broad backs into the sky, so much above the less animated clay of the wild below?

GILBERT WHITE, *from* Natural History of Selborne

ALL THESE THE LORD DID FRAME

The azured vault, the crystal circles bright,
The gleaming fiery torches powdered there;
The changing round, the shining beamy light,
The sad bearded fires, the monsters fair;
The prodigies appearing in the air;
The rearing thunders and the blustering winds;
The fowls in hue and shape and nature rare,
The pretty notes that winged musicians finds;
In earth, the savoury flowers, the metalled minds,
The wholesome herbs, the hautie pleasant trees,
The silver streams, the beasts of sundry kinds,
The bounded roars and fishes of the seas,—
    All these, for teaching man, the Lord did frame
    To do his will whose glory shines in thame.

KING JAMES I, *from* The Lepanto, *1591*

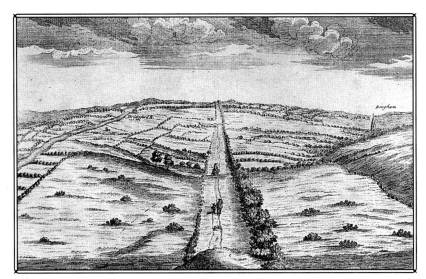

A Prospect . . . on the Foss, 7 September 1722, *from* Itinerarium Curiousum *by William Stukely*

6 October 1895

No sun, and much rain. In bed all day, groaning.

From the diary of GEORGE GISSING

THE YORKSHIRE DALES

S UCH IS THE LANDSCAPE I SEE WHEN I THINK OF THE DALES. This stony road has grown from 'the little and the lone green lane' that leads down from the moor. The late sunlight is flowing down the valley and seems at once to magnify and mellow every feature of the scene. Most surely of all it distinguishes the stone field walls that run across the valley, dipping down in full curves from cliff to bottom, interrupted by the tree-grown meander of the river, then rising again in equal curves to meet the opposite cliff. The long green lining of the dale is striped by these transverse bars, part stone, part softer shadow. The walls, built by hands with millions of fragments from the limestone hills, seem a calm assertion of the successful labour of generations, of the conquest of this hard Pennine realm. Every stone, with its own immense history held in it, has been handled, judged, given its chink to fill in a plan seen not on paper but freely in the builder's mind. Scattered among the fields, throwing angular shadows, are the neat stone sheds which the dalesmen build far above their farms, and where they keep some hay and milk their cows in a richly-smelling gloom. At this moment, with iron-shod boots ringing on the stony track, fresh from milking a man passes with a zinc budget strapped to his back. I can hear the milk slapping against the sides of the can. Following him down with my eyes I see that the valley bottom is filling with shadows, the wall bars are growing faint and the clustered village is steeped for a moment in a paradisaical rose light before that, too, turns grey, a fading ash. I look straight at the sun that is causing this havoc, see it as a bulging, sagging mass on the lip of the pass, then it is gone, leaving only a dancing green spot on my inner eye.

JACQUETTA HAWKES, *from* Prospect of Britain

MY SISTER EMILY LOVED THE MOORS. FLOWERS BRIGHTER than the rose bloomed in the blackest of the heath for her; out of a sullen hollow in a livid hill-side her mind could make an Eden. She found in the bleak solitude many and dear delights; and not the least and best loved was— liberty.

Liberty was the breath of Emily's nostrils; without it, she perished. The change from her own home to a school, and from her own very noiseless, very secluded, but unrestricted and inartificial mode of life, to one of disciplined routine (though under the kindliest auspices) was what she failed in enduring. Her nature proved here too strong for her fortitude. Every morning when she woke, the vision of home and the moors rushed on her, and darkened and saddened the day that lay before her. Nobody knew what ailed her but me—I knew only too well.

CHARLOTTE BRONTË, *from* Memoir of Emily Brontë

High waving heather, 'neath stormy blasts bending,
Midnight and moonlight and bright shining stars;
Darkness and glory rejoicingly blending,
Earth rising to heaven and heaven descending,
Man's spirit away from its drear dongeon sending,
Bursting the fetters and breaking the bars.

All down the mountain sides, wild forests lending
One mighty voice to the life-giving wind;
Rivers their banks in the jubilee rending,
Fast through the valleys a reckless course wending,
Wider and deeper their waters extending,
Leaving a desolate desert behind.

Shining and lowering and swelling and dying,
Changing for ever from midnight to noon;
Roaring like thunder, like soft music sighing,
Shadows on shadows advancing and flying,
Lightning-bright flashes the deep gloom defying,
Coming as swiftly and fading as soon.

EMILY BRONTË

18 May 1874

BRIGHT. TOOK BR TOURNADE TO COMBE WOOD TO SEE and gather bluebells, which we did, but fell in blue-handed with a gamekeeper, which is a humbling thing to do. Then we heard a nightingale utter a few strains – strings of very liquid gurgles.

On the way home, from about 4.30 to 5 p.m. but no doubt longer, were two taper tufts of vapour or cloud in shape like the tufts in ermine, say, touched with red on the inside, bluish at the outer and tapering end, stood on each side of the sun at the distance, I think, the halo stands at and as if flying outward from the halo. The left-hand one was long-tailed and curved slightly upwards. They were not quite diametrically opposite but a little above the horizontal diameter and seemed to radiate towards the sun. I have seen the phenomenon before.

From the diary of GERARD MANLEY HOPKINS

From DUN-COLOUR

The dry vermilion glow of familiar red breast
Is not his real glory: that is the greenish,
Light-toned, light-dissembling, eye-deceiving
Dun of his smooth-sloped back, and on his belly
The whitish dun is laid to deceive the shadow:
In the dear linnet the olive-dun is lovely,
And the primrose-duns in the yellowhammer: but most
   beguiling,
Perhaps because of the perfect shape, is the ash-dun
The quietest, most urbane, unprofaneable colour
Reserved as her livery of beauty to the hedge-sparrow.
There is a royal azure in her blood,
As her eggs prove, and in her nature gold,
For her children's throats are kingcups; but she veils them,
Mingled and blended, in her rare dun-colour.

For the rose-duns, and the blue-duns, look to the finches,
For the clean clear brown-duns, to the fallow deer
(How the sudden tear smarts in the eye wearied of cities)
And for all these and more to the many toadstools,
Which alone have the violet-dun, livid yet lovely.

RUTH PITTER

16 June 1789

THE SWEETEST SOFTEST SILENT NIGHT. CLOUDS TO THE West of a gleaming red. We leaned over the gate, admiring the solemnity of the scene and the profound Silence which reigned around as if we were the only inhabitants of this sweet Valley. Suddenly we heard a sweet pipe. Enquired who was the Performer. 'Thomas Jones the Glazier is playing on the Wall of the Churchyard which is over the Dee.' We listened till the Village struck ten.

From the diary of LADY ELEANOR BUTLER

SOLITUDE

Happy the man, whose wish and care
A few paternal acres bound,
Content to breathe his native air
   In his own ground.

Whose herds with milk, whose fields with bread,
Whose flocks supply him with attire;
Whose trees in summer yield him shade,
   In winter fire.

Blest, who can unconcernedly find
Hours, days, and years, slide soft away
In health of body, peace of mind;
   Quiet by day.

Sound sleep by night; study and ease
Together mixed, sweet recreation,
And innocence, which most does please
   With meditation.

Thus let me live, unseen, unknown;
Thus unlamented let me die;
Steal from the world, and not a stone
   Tell where I lie.

ALEXANDER POPE

LOVE

THE PASSIONATE SHEPHERD
TO HIS LOVE

Come live with me and be my Love,
And we will all the pleasures prove
That hills and valleys, dales and fields,
Or woods or steepy mountain yields.

And we will sit upon the rocks,
And see the shepherds feed their flocks
By shallow rivers, to whose falls
Melodious birds sing madrigals.

And I will make thee beds of roses
And a thousand fragrant posies;
A cap of flowers, and a kirtle
Embroider'd all with leaves of myrtle.

A gown made of the finest wool
Which from our pretty lambs we pull;
Fair-linèd slippers for the cold,
With buckles of the purest gold.

A belt of straw and ivy-buds
With coral clasps and amber studs:
And if these pleasures may thee move,
Come live with me and be my Love.

The shepherd swains shall dance and sing
For thy delight each May morning:
If these delights thy mind may move,
Then live with me and be my Love.

CHRISTOPHER MARLOWE

THE WIFE'S LAMENT

I MAKE THIS SONG OF MY DEEP SADNESS, OF MY OWN LOT. I can say that since I grew up I have not endured miseries new or old more than now. Ever I suffer the torment of my exile. First my lord went hence from his people over the tossing waves. I had sorrow at dawn as to where in the land my lord might be. Then I set out, a friendless exile, to seek helpers in my woeful hard straits. The man's kinsmen began to plot in secret thought to part us, so that we should live most wretchedly, most widely sundered in the world, and a yearning came upon me. My lord bade me take up my dwelling here; few dear loyal friends had I in this place; and so my mind is sad, since I found the man most mated to me unhappy, sad in heart, cloaking his mind, plotting mischief with blithe manner. Full often we two pledged one another that naught but death should divide us; that is changed now. Our friendship now is as if it had not been. I must needs endure the hate of my dear one far and near. They bade me dwell in the forest grove under the oak-tree in the earth-cave. Old is this earth-hall; I am filled with yearning. Dim are the valleys, high the hills, harsh strongholds o'ergrown with briers, dwellings empty of joy. Full often the departure of my lord has seized cruelly upon me. There are loving friends alive on the earth; they have their bed; while alone at dawn I pass through this earth-cave to beneath the oak-tree, where I sit a long summer's day. There I can mourn my miseries, many hardships, for I can never calm my care of mind, nor all that longing which has come upon me in this life.

ANON, *from the Anglo-Saxon*

THE DAY ROSIE BURDOCK DECIDED TO TAKE ME IN HAND was a motionless day of summer, creamy, hazy and amber-coloured, with the beech trees standing in heavy sunlight as though clogged with wild wet honey. It was the time of haymaking, so when we came out of school Jack and I went to the farm to help.

The whirr of the mower met us across the stubble, rabbits jumped like firecrackers about the fields, and the hay smelt crisp and sweet. The farmer's men were all hard at work, raking, turning and loading. Tall, whiskered fellows forked the grass, their chests like bramble patches. The air swung with their forks and the swathes took wing and rose like eagles to the tops of the wagons. The farmer gave us a short fork each and we both pitched in with the rest . . .

I stumbled on Rosie behind a haycock, and she grinned up at me with the sly, glittering eyes of her mother. She wore her tartan frock and cheap brass necklace, and her bare legs were brown with hay-dust.

'Get out a there,' I said. 'Go on.'

Rosie had grown and was hefty now, and I was terrified of her. In her cat-like eyes and curling mouth I saw unnatural wisdoms more threatening than anything I could imagine. The last time we'd met I'd hit her with a cabbage stump. She bore me no grudge, just grinned.

'I got summat to show ya.'

'You push off,' I said.

I felt dry and dripping, icy hot. Her eyes glinted, and I stood rooted. Her face was wrapped in a pulsating haze and her body seemed to flicker with lightning.

'You thirsty?' she said.

'I ain't, so there.'

'You be,' she said. 'C'mon.'

So I stuck the fork into the ringing ground and followed her, like doom.

We went a long way, to the bottom of the field, where a wagon stood half-loaded. Festoons of untrimmed grass hung down like curtains all around it. We crawled underneath, between the wheels, into a herb-scented cave of darkness. Rosie scratched about, turned over a sack, and revealed a stone jar of cider.

'It's cider,' she said. 'You ain't to drink it though. Not much of it, any rate.'

Huge and squat, the jar lay on the grass like an unexploded bomb. We lifted it up, unscrewed the stopper, and smelt the whiff of fermented apples. I held the jar to my mouth and rolled my eyes sideways, like a beast at a waterhole. 'Go on,' said Rosie. I took a deep breath . . .

Never to be forgotten, that first long secret drink of golden fire, juice of those valleys and of that time, wine of wild orchards, of russet summer, of plump red apples and Rosie's burning cheeks. Never to be forgotten, or ever tasted again . . .

LAURIE LEE, *from* Cider with Rosie

THE UNQUIET GRAVE

The wind doth blow today, my love,
   And a few small drops of rain.
I never had but one true-love,
   In cold grave she was lain.

I'll do as much for my true-love
   As any young man may,
I'll sit and mourn all at her grave
   For a twelvemonth and a day.

The twelvemonth and a day being up,
   The dead began to speak:
Oh who sits weeping on my grave,
   And will not let me sleep?

'Tis I, my love, sits on your grave,
   And will not let you sleep,
For I crave one kiss of your clay-cold lips.
   And that is all I seek.

You crave one kiss of my clay-cold lips,
   But my breath smells earthy strong.
If you have one kiss of my clay-cold lips,
   Your time will not be long.

'Tis down in yonder garden green,
   Love, where we used to walk,
The finest flower that ere was seen
   Is withered to a stalk.

The stalk is withered dry, my love,
   So will our hearts decay.
So make yourself content, my love,
   Till God calls you away.

ANON

6 August 1872

MRS PRING WAS MARRIED TO JAMES ROGER LAST Tuesday as quietly as possible. She would not allow the church bells to be rung though the ringers entreated her to let them ring a peal, and she openly wished for rain so that no-one might be able to come to the wedding. Moreover she invited as few people as possible to the wedding dinner (not even her own mother-in-law) that she might not cause Mr and Mrs Venables any needless expense. It was with great difficulty that she was prevailed upon to go to Brecon for the night and to let her husband accompany her. Her wish was that the bridegroom should return to his own house while she slept at the Vicarage as usual. She said she did not want any of that fuss and nonsense. She looked upon marriage as a religious thing. But Mrs Venables represented to her what a talk would be caused by such a proceeding, so she consented to go to Brecon for one night as a bride and let the bridegroom go too.

From the diary of THE REVEREND FRANCIS KILVERT

THE FOGGY, FOGGY DEW

When I was a bachelor I lived all alone
   And I worked at the weaver's trade,
And the only, only thing that I ever did wrong
   Was to woo a fair young maid.

I wooed her in the winter time,
   And in the summer too,
And the only, only thing that I ever did wrong
   Was to keep her from the foggy foggy dew.

One night she came to my bedside
   When I was fast asleep,
She flung her arms around my neck
   And she began to weep.

She wept, she cried, she damn near died,
   She said, What can I do?
So I rolled her into bed and I covered up her head,
   Just to keep her from the foggy foggy dew.

O I am a bachelor, I live with my son
   And we work at the weaver's trade,
And every single time that I look into his eyes
   He reminds me of that fair young maid.

He reminds me of the winter time
   And of the summer too,
And of the many, many times I held her in my arms
   Just to keep her from the foggy foggy dew.

ANON

OPPOSITE: The
Lost Path,
engraving after the
painting by
Frederick Walker,
1869

O NE TIME, HOWEVER, WE WERE NEAR QUARRELLING. HE said the pleasantest manner of spending a hot July day was lying from morning till evening on a bank of heath in the middle of the moors, with the bees humming dreamily about among the bloom, and the larks singing high up overhead, and the blue sky and bright sun shining steadily and cloudlessly. That was his most perfect idea of heaven's happiness: mine was rocking in a rustling green tree, with a west wind blowing, and bright white clouds flitting rapidly above; and not only larks, but throstles, and blackbirds, and linnets, and cuckoos pouring out music on every side, and the moors seen at a distance, broken into cool dusky dells; but close by great swells of long grass undulating in waves to the breeze; and woods and sounding water, and the whole world awake and wild with joy. He wanted all to lie in an ecstasy of peace; I wanted all to sparkle and dance in a glorious jubilee. I said his heaven would be only half alive; and he said mine would be drunk: I said I should fall asleep in his; and he said he could not breathe in mine, and began to grow very snappish. At last, we agreed to try both, as soon as the right weather came; and then we kissed each other and were friends.'

EMILY BRONTË, *from* Wuthering Heights

SILENT NOON

Your hands lie open in the long fresh grass,
The finger-points look through like rosy blooms;
Your eyes smile peace. The pasture gleams and glooms
'Neath billowing skies that scatter and amass.
All round our nest, far as the eye can pass,
Are golden kingcup-fields with silver edge
Where the cow-parsley skirts the hawthorn-hedge.
'Tis visible silence, still as the hour-glass.
Deep in the sun-searched growths the dragon-fly
Hangs like a blue thread loosened from the sky—

So this winged hour is dropt to us from above.
Oh! clasp we to our hearts, for deathless dower,
This close-companioned inarticulate hour
When twofold silence was the song of love.

DANTE GABRIEL ROSSETTI

3 July 1765

I HAVE BEEN SO EMBARRASSED WITH A MULTIPLICITY OF business, that I was not able to continue my journal, being, on the 19th day of June, married, at our church, to Mary Hicks, servant to Luke Spence, Esq., of South Malling, by the Rev. Mr Porter; and for about fourteen days was very ill with a tertian ague, or, rather, an intermitting fever; then the ceremony of receiving visitors, and again the returning of them, has indeed, together with the business of my trade, taking up so much of my time, that I was obliged to omit that which would have given me the greatest pleasure imaginable to have continued; but, however, thank God, I begin once more to be a little settled, and am happy in my choice. I have, it's true, not married a learned lady, nor is she a gay one; but I trust she is good-natured, and one that will use her utmost endeavour to make me happy. As to her fortune, I shall one day have something considerable, and there seems to be rather a flowing stream. Well, here let us drop the subject, and begin a new one.

From the diary of THOMAS TURNER

Roses, their sharp spines being gone,
Not royal in their smells alone,
   But in their hue;
Maiden pinks, of odour faint,
Daisies smell-less, yet most quaint,
   And sweet thyme true.

Primrose, first-born child of Ver,
Merry spring-time's harbinger,
   With her bells dim;
Oxlips in their cradles growing,
Marigolds on death-beds blowing,
   Larks'-heels trim;

All dear Nature's children sweet,
Lie 'fore bride and bridegroom's feet,
   Blessing their sense;
Not an angel of the air,
Bird melodious, or bird fair,
   Is absent hence.

The crow, the sland'rous cuckoo, nor
The boding raven, nor chough hoar,
   Nor chatt'ring pie,
May on our bridehouse perch or sing,
Or with them any discord bring,
   But from it fly.

WILLIAM SHAKESPEARE, *from* The Two Noble Kinsmen

OPPOSITE: *Kissing
cousins at a fête,
Yately, c. 1920*

BIRD IN A CAGE

As I went out one May morning
   To hear the birds so sweet,
I hid myself in a green shady dell
   And watched two lovers meet.

You courted me, was what she said,
   Till you got me to comply.
You courted me with a merry mood,
   All night with you I lie.

And when your heart was mine, false love,
   And your head lay on my breast,
You could make me believe by the fall of your arm
   That the sun rose in the west.

I wish your breast was made of glass
   That all in it might behold,
I'd write our secret in your breast
   In letters made of gold.

There's many a girl can go about
   And hear the birds so sweet,
While I, poor girl, must stay alone
   And rock my cradle and weep.

There's many a star shall dwindle in the west,
   There's many a leaf below,
There's many a curse shall light on a man
   For treating a poor girl so.

Oh I can sing as lonely a song
   As any little bird in a cage,
Who twelve long months astray have been gone,
   And scarce fifteen of age.

ANON

58

O MY BELLY

O my belly, my belly, John Trench!
What's the matter with your belly, my wench?
Som'at in my belly goes niddity-nod,
What can it be, good God, good God.

ANON

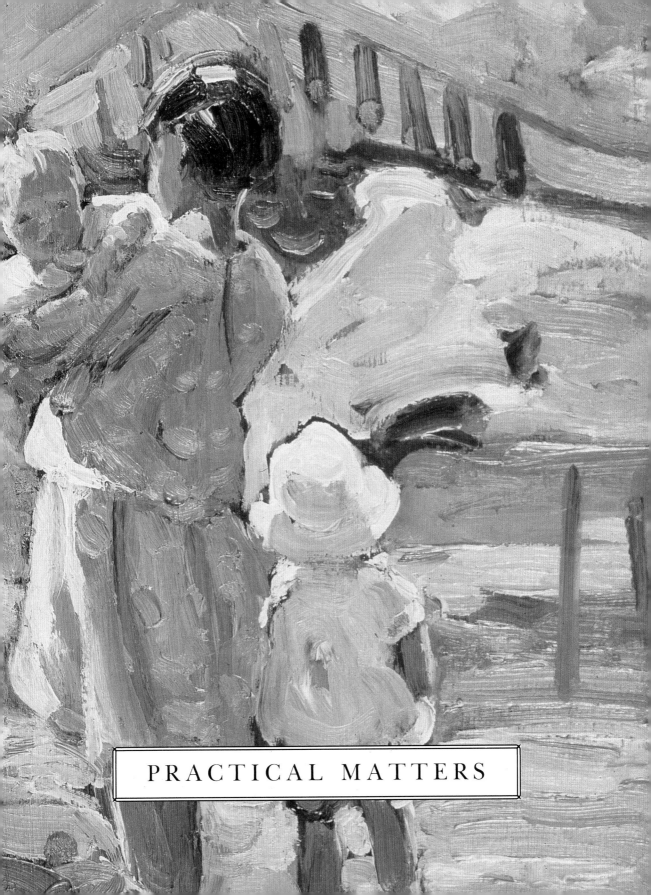

PRACTICAL MATTERS

4 October 1788

That little Dirty village quack sent in his Bill. Never paid money with more reluctance.

From the diary of LADY ELEANOR BUTLER

B UT TESS SET TO WORK. PATIENCE, THAT BLENDING OF moral courage with physical timidity, was now no longer a minor feature in Mrs Angel Clare; and it sustained her.

The swede-field in which she and her companion were set hacking was a stretch of a hundred odd acres, in one patch, on the highest ground of the farm, rising above stony lanchets or lynchets – the outcrop of siliceous veins in the chalk formation, composed of myriads of loose white flints in bulbous, cusped, and phallic shapes. The upper half of each turnip had been eaten off by the live-stock, and it was the business of the two women to grub up the lower or earthy half of the root with a hooked fork called a hacker, that it might be eaten also. Every leaf of the vegetable having already been consumed, the whole field was in colour a desolate drab; it was a complexion without features, as if a face, from chin to brow, should be only an expanse of skin. The sky wore, in another colour, the same likeness; a white vacuity of countenance with the lineaments gone. So these two upper and nether visages confronted each other all day long, the white face looking down on the brown face, and the brown face looking up at the white face, without anything standing between them but the two girls crawling over the surface of the former like flies.

Nobody came near them, and their movements showed a mechanical regularity; their forms standing enshrouded in Hessian 'wroppers' – sleeved brown pinafores, tied behind to the bottom, to keep their gowns from blowing about – scant skirts revealing boots that reached high up the ankles, and yellow sheepskin gloves with gauntlets. The pensive character which the curtained hood lent to their bent heads would have reminded the observer of some early Italian conception of the two Marys.

They worked on hour after hour, unconscious of the forlorn aspect they bore in the landscape, not thinking of the justice or injustice of their lot. Even in such a position as theirs it was possible to exist in a dream. In the afternoon the rain came on again, and Marian said that they need not work any more. But if they did not work they would not be paid; so they worked on.

THOMAS HARDY, *from* Tess of the D'Urbervilles

NO DOUBT EVEN THE MINOR COUNTIES HAVE THEIR charms; and each, too, boasts its own scenery, tradition, accent and wares. An interesting old list of the last, *i.e.* their 'natural commodities' – is given by Thomas Fuller in his *Worthies* [1672]. Here is a selection:

Cumberland	Pearls, Black-lead and Copper.
Hampshire	Red Deer, Honey, Wax and Hogs.
Cambridgeshire	Eeels, Hares, Saffron and Willows.
Cornwall	Diamonds, Ambergris, ('sweetest of gums'), Garlic ('most stinking of roots'), Pilchards, Slate and Tin.
Lincolnshire	Pikes, Wild-fowl, Feathers and Pippins.
Somerset	Lead, Cheese, Mastiffs, Woad ('a deep black tincture' – with which our British ancestors blued themselves), 'and that *Lapis Calaminaris* which, added to copper, makes brass.'
Surrey	Fuller's Earth, Walnuts and Box.
Warwickshire	Sheep, Ash and Coal.
Sussex	Iron, Wheatears, Carps and Talc.
Worcestershire	Lampreys, Perry and Salt.
Yorkshire	Geat [Jet], Alum, Lime and Horses.
Northamptonshire	Saltpetre and Pigeons.

Nottinghamshire	Liquorice.
Staffordshire	Nails.
Wiltshire	Wool.

And last, but still first, beloved *Kent,* with her Morello Cherries, her Flaze, Saint Foine, Madder and Trouts.

> And though myn English be sympill to myn entent,
> Hold me excusid, for I was borne in Kent.

WALTER DE LA MARE, *from* Come Hither

L AST NIGHT WE HAD A TRAGEDY. THE SHEEP, HAVING finished No. 11, were penned upon a little stretch of grass (not more than an acre in extent) that is separated from it by a fence which it is proposed to remove, laying drainage pipes in the ditch and filling it up, so soon as we can find time for the task. I must explain that among the movable hurdles, which are of iron and mounted upon wheels, is what is known as a lamb-hurdle – that is, an ingenious contrivance fitted with rollers set horizontally, too narrow to admit of the passage of ewes, but large enough to allow the lambs to pass in and out of the fold, as they do not grow well if kept constantly confined with their mothers. Doubtless some of these wandered out in the darkness, and while they were thus away from the ewes, that could not go to protect them – as they will do with great courage if free – were attacked by a dog or dogs. The ravening brute, or brutes, seized one of the lambs – the finest that I have – and murdered it. In the morning it was found lying in the holl, its throat torn completely out and half the head eaten, a dreadful and a piteous sight.

Another lamb was also badly bitten in the leg, but managed to escape back into the fold. Both of these had been sold to the butcher for twenty-nine shillings each, on the understanding that he was to take them when it suited him; but as they had not been delivered, of course I am liable for the loss.

H. RIDER HAGGARD, *from* A Farmer's Year

A sheepfold, from the Luttrell Psalter, *fourteenth century*

21 March 1787

THE SEVEN YEAR OLD HOWICK OX WAS KILLED AT Alnwick, amazingly fat, and weighed as follows: the carcase 152st 8lbs, the tallow 16st = 168st 8lbs. Bolton and Embleton, butchers. The head and feet of this ox were not weighed. It was sold at tenpence per pound, in pieces, and stakes of it at one shilling; calculated to have sold, adding every article together, for the sum of £100 or thereabouts. Very remarkable to be fed in Northumberland.

From the diary of NICHOLAS BROWN

THIS WAS THE BEGINNING OF HER LONG INTEREST IN Herdwick sheep, the little hardy blue-fleeced pretty-faced mountain sheep indigenous to the fells. From the first moment of seeing the native fell flocks, which had bred among the high crags – so far as anyone knew – since before the Stone Age, their ancient hardihood touched her.

'Cool is the air above the craggy summit,' she makes the old sheep say, in the story which was to become a chapter of *The Fairy Caravan*; 'clear is the water of the mountain keld . . . What though the tempest sweeps the fell in winter – through tempest, frost or heat, we live our patient day's allotted span. Wild and free as when the stonemen told our puzzled early numbers; untamed as when the Norsemen named our grassings in their stride. Our little feet had ridged the slopes before the passing Romans. On through the fleeting centuries, when fresh blood came from Iceland, Spain or Scotland – stubborn, unchanged, *unbeaten* – we have held the stony waste.' This lonely farm, covering the Troutbeck valley and the surrounding heights, now became the centre of her farming life, providing strong draughts of space and solitude, nourishing her imagination. It was about twelve miles from Sawrey, but in any weather her car might be seen winding along the valley road, or her short stout indomitable figure making its way on foot slowly and alone to the top of Troutbeck Tongue or Lowther Brow, where the goat-footed flocks were feeding along the crags. She would spend whole days alone on the hills like this, eating her bread and cheese under a boulder, or, if it rained, at 'High Buildings', a stone shelter that the lambing-time shepherds used.

MARGARET LANE, from The Tale of Beatrix Potter

28 September 1837

AN ESCAPE TOOK PLACE FROM THE STOW WORKHOUSE LAST night: a blind sailor having eloped with a female pauper who has left behind her two bastard children. In the present unfinished state of the new workhouse the parties had found an opportunity of communicating with each other. But these are daily lessening so that in a day or two their project would have been baffled by additional locks and bars. In the course of the night each stole from their respective dormitories . . . and both escaped. I gave instructions to the police to look out for the runaways. The woman has left her two children chargeable and has therefore committed a felony and an act of vagrancy.

From the diary of THE REVEREND FRANCIS WITTS

COUNTRY STATUTES

Come all you lads of high renown and listen to my story,
For now the time is coming on that is all to your glory;
For Jumping Joan is coming here the statutes to admire,
To see the lads and lasses standing waiting to be hired.

So to the hirings we have come, all for to look for places,
If with the master we agree and he will give good wages.

The master that a servant wants will now stand in a wonder;
You all must ask ten pounds a year and none of you go under.
It's you that must do all the work, and what they do require,
So now stand up for wages, lads, before that you do hire.

There's rolling Gin the hemp will spin and Sal will mind the dairy,
And John will kiss his mistress when the master he is weary.
There's Tom and Joe will reap and mow; they'll thrash and ne'er
  be tired;
They'll load the cart and do their part, so they're the lads to hire.

The farmer's wife so full of pride must have a lady's maid,
All for to dress and curl her hair and powder it beside;
But the girl of heart to dress so smart, they call her charming Nancy,
She can wink and blink in such a style, she's all the young men's fancy.

And when the mop it is all o'er, you that are young and hearty
Must take your girl all in your hand and join a drinking party;
But when you are returning home, enjoying sweet embraces,
With love and honour spend the night at statutes, fairs and
    races.

ANON

20 October 1830

STAFFORDSHIRE SESSIONS. A REMARKABLE WARM DAY. I FELT it quite uncomfortable as I rode Roany, who was ever a rough goer. A very full bench of magistrates, and a full bar of prisoners. No crimes of great magnitude, and crime will certainly increase from the effect of the new Beer Bill, which came into operation on the 18th. The state of the country is sufficiently demoralized without further incitement; and the effect of the Beer Bill must, to a certainty, add to the licentiousness of the populace, by affording them the means to be dissolute, from the readily obtaining sufficient to get drink at a cheap rate. Licensing Ale Shops in every village, which must become a rendezvous for vice in all its bearings!

From the diary of GENERAL WILLIAM DYOTT

21 March — Landlord and Tenant

JOHN ODY WAS CLEANING OUT HIS FOWL-HOUSE: AN old-fashioned wooden fowl-house sheltering old-fashioned hens; he had a rusty wheelbarrow and an ancient prong. The barns look tottery, ivy grips the stone tiles of outhouses, pig-sties are falling in. There's a hand-pump just inside the back door, an outside privy, and electricity is the only new-fangled device that's been installed.

I asked him if his hens paid. 'Lord bless you no, if I got twice the price for my eggs it still wouldn't cover the cost of their feed.' Then why keep them? 'Well, the Colonel likes the eggs, he'd be disappointed.' The Colonel is the landlord, the man who, according to the book, should have had water laid on, yards concreted, buildings modernized and so on. Far from complaining, the tenant is well satisfied with his *quid pro quo*.

'He's been fair to me. He's not gone putting up the rent every year or two like most.' In fact, I believe he hasn't put up the rent at all, which must be a unique situation. So everyone's happy, more or less pretending that the twentieth century hasn't happened.

Things haven't always run so smoothly between landlord and tenant. When John Ody first came, he and the Colonel fell out over some timber and didn't speak for five years. Then a day came when, passing each other in the lane, the Colonel nodded. A year or so later he said 'good-morning'; matters progressed, and now they're on excellent terms.

ELSPETH HUXLEY, *from* Gallipot Eyes

1 January 1805

WITH THE SMALL PITTANCE THEY OBTAIN EACH WEEK BY the sweat of their brow much is to be done. Not only only bread to be purchased (their chief food) but candle, soap, thread &c; all, too, necessarily bought at the little shop near them at double price – and besides this a part of their earnings must be put by towards the payment of the year's rent (which often amounts to three or four pounds, though they frequently cannot get their landlords to keep their tenements in reasonable repair). Some money, too, must be reserved for a purchase of shoes or other indispensable articles of clothing . . . A strong pair of poor man's shoes comes to no less than fourteen shillings; and the addition of tipping and nailing, to make them serviceable for labour in the field &c, is eighteen pence more. An inferior kind, which have not half the wear, comes to nine shillings and sixpence and the tipping to four-teen pence. I have heard, with management, the stronger sort will last a year. A carter's frock costs ten shillings. A pair of ordinary worsted stockings is four shillings and now very small balls of worsted for mending them costs as much as four pence. A shirt of dowlass at 22d a yard comes to six and sixpence. A woman's coloured checked apron cannot be got under five shillings. The cheapest stuff of eight pence a yard for a gown, with the coarsest body lining, is eight shillings and, after all, is too coarse and slight to be any wear for a working person . . . A common linsey petticoat comes to seven shillings and all other things in proportion; and yearly the price of each article is raised. Do not the poor seem to be making bricks without straw in procuring for themselves any thing like decency of apparel?

From the diary of PENELOPE HIND

AUG 17. BEGUN SHEARING MY WHEAT THIS MORNING AND gave the shearers according to the Norfolk custom as under, a good breakfast, at 11 o'clock plumb cakes with carraway seeds in them, and some Liquor, a good dinner with plumb Puddings and at 4 beer again. NB the above are called elevens and fours.

From the diary of THE REVEREND JAMES WOODFORDE

SUMMER

SUMMER IS PERFECT NOW.

The wheat says so, when in the dawn it drips with half an hour's rain and gleams like copper under the fresh, dim sky; it cries aloud the same when it crackles in the midday sun, and the golden sea of it washes murmurously to the feet of the hills.

In the hedges and fields the agrimony wands and mullein staves, the climbing vetch, the cushioned bird's-foot lotus, the myriads of ragwort and sow-thistle, are golden too.

The meadowsweet and honeysuckle flowers and the wild carrot seeds give out sweet scents, but not so strong as not to be drowned, when the wind blows, by a thousand lesser scents from field and wood and farmyard.

Wood-pigeons coo in the high-shaded storeys of the beeches and in the wet willow copses where bushes and herbage have grown so dense that hardly a bird's-nester or a lover would care to penetrate them. In the dark wood alleys, all day long, hang insects whose wings seem to be still in their swiftness, like golden lamps.

EDWARD THOMAS, *from* Through the Year

SONG

How sweet I roamed from field to field
And tasted all the summer's pride,
Till I the Prince of Love beheld
Who in the sunny beams did glide!

He showed me lilies for my hair,
And blushing roses for my brow;
He led me through his gardens fair
Where all his golden pleasures grow.

With sweet May dews my wings were wet,
And Phoebus fired my vocal rage;

He caught me in his silken net,
And shut me in his golden cage.

He loves to sit and hear me sing,
Then, laughing, sports and plays with me;
Then stretches out my golden wing,
And mocks my loss of liberty.

WILLIAM BLAKE

SUMMER WAS ALSO THE TIME OF THESE: OF SUDDEN PLENTY, of slow hours and actions, of diamond haze and dust on the eyes, of the valley in post-vernal slumber; of burying birds out of seething corruption; of Mother sleeping heavily at noon; of jazzing wasps and dragonflies, haystooks and thistle-seeds, snows of white butterflies, skylarks' eggs, bee-orchids and frantic ants; of wolf-cub parades, and boy-scout's bugles; of sweat running down the legs; of boiling potatoes on bramble fires, of flames glass-blue in the sun; of lying naked in the hill-cold stream; begging pennies for bottles of pop; of girls' bare arms and unripe cherries, green apples and liquid walnuts; of fights and falls and new-scabbed knees, sobbing pursuits and flights; of picnics high up in the crumbling quarries, of butter running like oil, of sunstroke, fever, and cucumber peel stuck cool to one's burning brow. All this, and the feeling that it would never end, that such days had come for ever, with the pump drying up and the water-butt crawling, and the chalk ground hard as the moon. All sights twice-brilliant and smells twice-sharp, all game-days twice as long. Double charged as we were, like the meadow ants, with the frenzy of the sun, we used up the light to its last violet drop, and even then couldn't go to bed.

When darkness fell, and the huge moon rose, we stirred to a second life. Then boys went calling along the roads, wild slit-eyed animal calls, Walt Kerry's naked nasal yodel, Boney's jackal scream. As soon as we heard them we crept outdoors, out

OPPOSITE:

Gathering lupins near Chichester, c. 1930

76

of our stifling bedrooms, stepped out into moonlight warm as the sun to join our chalk-white, moon-masked gang.

Games in the moon. Games of pursuit and capture. Games that the night demanded. Best of all, Fox and Hounds – go where you like, and the whole of the valley to hunt through. Two chosen boys loped away through the trees and were immediately swallowed in shadow. We gave them five minutes, then set off after them. They had churchyard, farmyard, barns, quarries, hilltops and woods to run to. They had all night, and the whole of the moon, and five miles of country to hide in . . .

LAURIE LEE, *from* Cider with Rosie

25 July 1954

INCESSANT DRENCHING RAIN, BEATING AND SOAKING. THE madonna lilies lie prostrate; it is disgustingly cold. Lord what a summer!

From the diary of FRANCES PARTRIDGE

SUMMER DAWN

Pray but one prayer for me 'twixt thy closed lips;
  Think but one thought of me up in the stars.
The summer night waneth, the morning light slips,
  Faint and grey 'twixt the leaves of the aspen,
    betwixt the cloud-bars,
That are patiently waiting there for the dawn:
  Patient and colourless, though Heaven's gold
Waits to float through them along with the sun.
Far out in the meadows, above the young corn,
  The heavy elms wait, and restless and cold

The uneasy wind rises; the roses are dun;
Through the long twilight they pray for the dawn,
Round the lone house in the midst of the corn.
Speak but one word to me over the corn,
Over the tender, bowed locks of the corn.

WILLIAM MORRIS

18 May 1943

TODAY I AM BY THE RIVER BELOW EAST PECKHAM. I'M writing letters, roasting in the sun, sweating, burning, turning red. The feathers of the grass tickle me and I am almost stupefied. Oh, how lovely it is. Bang in front is a concrete pill-box covered with nets, slowly being swallowed up by weeds. *They'll* win, every time.

From the diary of DENTON WELCH

31 August 1928

THIS IS THE LAST DAY OF AUGUST AND LIKE ALMOST ALL OF them of extraordinary beauty. Each day is fine enough and hot enough for sitting out; but also full of wandering clouds; and that fading and rising of the light which so enraptures me in the downs; which I am always comparing to the light beneath an alabaster bowl. The corn is now stood about in rows of three four or five solid shaped yellow cakes – rich, it seems, with eggs and spice; good to eat. Sometimes I see the cattle galloping 'like mad' as Dostoievsky would say, in the brooks. The clouds – if I could describe them I would; one yesterday had flowing hair on it, like the very fine white hair of an old man. At this moment they are white in a leaden sky; but

OVERLEAF:
Harvesters taking a break in the Thames Valley, pre-war

79

the sun behind the house, is making the grass green. I walked to the racecourse today and saw a weasel.

From the diary of VIRGINIA WOOLF

LONG LION DAYS

Long lion days
Start with white haze
By midday you meet
A hammer of heat—
Whatever was sown
Now fully grown,
Whatever conceived
Now fully leaved,
Abounding, ablaze—
O long lion days!

PHILIP LARKIN

CHILDHOOD

I WAS VERY LOATH TO QUIT MY HOMELY PLEASURES FOR school, but at last I 'stood in lines' with the others in the playground. Of the first day I remember nothing; the picture in my mind of early school days is composite. I know I was small for my age, wiry and untiring; and that I wore a kilt and top, with an anchor worked in red on the sleeve, and a pinny to preserve my kilt from ill usage. My straight hair was parted at the side and tied on top with a ribbon, or it was combed back and worn with a ribbon like Alice.

The bell and the whistle were fun. Often we would play as far away from the school as possible; bell made us run towards school, whistle made us tear. I liked to play with May Gross and Francie Spears down Crooked Lane on a stile leading to Nicholls' Fields, or on a stone-heap down the same lane. This stone heap was perfect for playing 'mothers', as it afforded us material to build a fireplace in the sort of little house we made. The playground could just be reached if we waited for the bell at Nicholls' stile. In the girls' playground we stood in lines according to 'standards' or, on wet days, we played 'more sacks' in the lobby, until authority intervened. Then, to a tune on the piano, we marched, the girls by their door, and the boys by theirs, into the big room. On the boarded floor the boys in their hobnails made a sound like the trump of doom.

In the mornings we began with prayers and a well-sung hymn. I don't think any of us were in any doubt as to what we were supposed to be engaged in; whereas a little boy I know who went to a village school recently, and whose mind had been kept by his parents unprejudiced in the matter of the gods, reported on the first day that they had begun school with a funny game called 'Shut Eye'. The same child re-told the story of Adam and Eve to his little sister. 'And Dod said, "Now don't you touch that apple tree". And', very dramatically, 'they did. And Dod tame into the garden, and they hided away, and Dod said, "You tum out of that". And they tame out. And Dod said, "Now you do out of this". And they went out and' – long pause – 'they had ice-cream each'.

ANNE TRENEER, *from* School House in the Wind

SUMMONED BY BELLS

Nose! Smell again the early morning smells:
Congealing bacon and my father's pipe;
The after-breakfast freshness out of doors
Where sun had dried the heavy dew and freed
Acres of thyme to scent the links and lawns;
The rotten apples on our shady path
Where blowflies settled upon squashy heaps,
Intent and gorging; at the garden gate
Reek of Solignum on the wooden fence;
Mint round the spring, and fennel in the lane,
And honeysuckle wafted from the hedge;
The Lynams' cess-pool like a body-blow;
Then, clean, medicinal and cold – the sea.
'Breathe in the ozone, John. It's iodine.'
But which is iodine and which is drains?
Salt and hot sun on rubber water-wings . . .
Home to the luncheon smell of Irish stew
And washing-up stench from the kitchen sink
Because the sump is blocked. The afternoons
Brought coconut smell of gorse; at Mably's farm
Sweet smell of drying cowdung; then the moist
Exhaling of the earth in Shilla woods –
First earth encountered after days of sand.
Evening brought back the gummy smell of toys
And fishy stink of glue and Stickphast paste,
And sleep inside the laundriness of sheets.

JOHN BETJEMAN

THE CAT AND MY SECOND BROTHER WENT FISHING together for trout in the rivulet, puss always on a little boulder in the middle of the stream – at intervals putting her paws right into the water.

It was our first experience of a country life. We felt a quiet thankfulness and mild enjoyment, but being in impoverished circumstances could not take great delight in it. For the same reason we visited only two families in the neighbourhood. My sister and I were very noticeable, she dark and I fair, wearing our hair curling over our shoulders, well-dressed but in mourning. There were some wonderfully hot summers and we almost lived out of doors. Our dear old servant, Ann Chapell – the other, Elizabeth Mitchell left us – who was still with us following our fortunes in the good old style of servants. They kept a basket of crockery under a tree and a great kitchen table, and we had pleasant reading and working hours, and many meals there.

The garden's fruits were delicious – strange old apple trees with flavourings and names not now known. It bountifully rewarded my Father for his happy labours and greatly helped my Mother's housekeeping though she was always longing to get back to Plymouth, as indeed we all were.

EMMA HARDY, *from* Some Recollections

I N ONE OF MY MOTHER'S EARLY LETTERS THERE IS A SAD heart-cry: 'We are going to Down. Oh, you can't imagine how dull these English country-houses are! There is nothing at all to do there.' Down – now spelt Downe – in Kent, was my grandfather's house. He – Charles Darwin – had died in 1882, three years before I was born, and after his death my grandmother spent the winters in Cambridge and only the summers at Down House, where we all went for long visits. Sometimes, too, she lent us the house for the winter or spring holidays, so we knew the place well.

I am afraid it *was* dull for my mother, and probably would have been dull to most people . . .

But we Darwins never found it dull there, for we loved every moment of life in the country; and we all, old and young alike, were apt to fly away out of doors and windows, at the first sound of the front-door bell. 'Visitors! Danger!' would be the cry. I truly admire my mother for enduring so good-humouredly the long country holidays we spent at Down or in Yorkshire; for she did not care for the country for itself; people were her real interest. Prospects did not please her very much, but Man was far from being vile.

But to us, everything at Down was perfect. That was an axiom. And by us I mean, not only the children, but all the uncles and aunts who belonged there. Uncle Horace was once heard to say in a surprised voice: 'No, I don't really like salvias very much, *though they did grow at Down.*' The implication, to us, would have been obvious. Of course all the flowers that grew at Down were beautiful; and different from all other flowers. Everything there was different. And better.

For instance, the path in front of the veranda was made of large round water-worn pebbles, from some sea beach. They were not loose, but stuck down tight in moss and sand, and were black and shiny, as if they had been polished. I adored those pebbles. I mean literally, *adored*; worshipped. This passion made me feel quite sick sometimes. And it was adoration that I felt for the foxgloves at Down, and for the stiff red clay out of the Sandwalk clay-pit; and for the beautiful white paint on the nursery floor. This kind of feeling hits you in the stomach, and in the ends of your fingers, and it is probably the most important thing in life. Long after I have forgotten all my human loves, I shall still remember the smell of a gooseberry leaf, or the feel of the wet grass on my bare feet; or the pebbles in the path. In the long run it is this feeling that makes life worth living, this which is the driving force behind the artist's need to create.

Of course, there were things to worship everywhere. I can remember feeling quite desperate with love for the blisters in the dark red paint on the nursery window-sills at Cambridge, but at Down there were more things to worship than anywhere else in the world.

GWEN RAVERAT, *from* Period Piece

Mother and child,
1833

SKATING

. . . So through the darkness and the cold we flew,
And not a voice was idle; with the din
Smitten, the precipices rang aloud;
The leafless trees and every icy crag
Tinkled like iron; while far distant hills
Into the tumult sent an alien sound
Of melancholy not unnoticed, while the stars
Eastward were sparkling clear, and in the west
The orange sky of evening died away.
Not seldom from the uproar I retired
Into a silent bay, or sportively
Glanced sideway, leaving the tumultuous throng,
To cut across the reflex of a star
That fled, and, flying still before me, gleamed
Upon the glassy plain; and oftentimes,
When we had given our bodies to the wind,
And all the shadowy banks on either side
Came sweeping through the darkness, spinning still
In rapid line of motion, then at once
Have I, reclining back upon my heels,
Stopped short; yet still the solitary cliffs
Wheeled by me – even as if the earth had rolled

91

With visible motion her diurnal round!
Behind me did they stretch in solemn train,
Feebler and feebler, and I stood and watched
Till all was tranquil as a dreamless sleep . . .

WILLIAM WORDSWORTH

WE WENT TO THIS BOURN IN ORDER THAT I MIGHT SHOW my son the spot where I received the rudiments of my education. There is a little hop-garden in which I used to work when from eight to ten years old; from which I have scores of times run to follow the hounds, leaving the hoe to do the best that it could to destroy the weeds; but the most interesting thing was a *sand-hill*, which goes from a part of the heath down to the rivulet. As a due mixture of pleasure with toil, I, with two brothers, used occasionally to *disport* ourselves, as the lawyers call it, at this sand-hill. Our diversion was this: we used to go to the top of the hill, which was steeper than the roof of a house; one used to draw his arms out of the sleeves of his smock-frock, and lay himself down with his arms by his sides; and then the others, one at head, and the other at feet, sent him rolling down the hill like a barrel or a log of wood. By the time he got to the bottom, his hair, eyes, ears, nose, and mouth, were all full of this loose sand; then the others took their turn, and at every roll, there was a monstrous spell of laughter.

WILLIAM COBBETT, *from* Rural Rides

A BOY'S SONG

Where the pools are bright and deep,
Where the grey trout lies asleep,
Up the river and over the lea,
That's the way for Billy and me.

Where the blackbird sings the latest,
Where the hawthorn blooms the sweetest,
Where the nestlings chirp and flee,
That's the way for Billy and me.

Where the mowers mow the cleanest,
Where the hay lies thick and greenest,
There to track the homeward bee,
That's the way for Billy and me.

Where the hazel bank is steepest,
Where the shadow falls the deepest,
Where the clustering nuts fall free,
That's the way for Billy and me.

Why the boys should drive away
Little sweet maidens from their play,
Or love to banter and fight so well,
That's the thing I never could tell.

But this I know, I love to play
Through the meadow, among the hay;
Up the water and over the lea,
That's the way for Billy and me.

JAMES HOGG

11 January 1826

ALL IDEA OF STUDY IS DISSIPATED; THE BOYS TOOK THEIR gun and their skaites immediately after our breakfast and went to the basin at Bengrove, but as the snow had fallen in the night were obliged to employ sweepers. I went to see whether it was hard enough to bear them with safety. They did not arrive at Camerton till nearly dinner time, having spent the morning in shooting. I regret the gun was purchased, as it has been a sad obstacle to reading; indeed, it seems now considered that nothing more is to be done in the way of study this vacation. When once the bow is unloosed it is difficult to new string it again.

From the diary of THE REVEREND JOHN SKINNER

I
N THE OTHER HALF OF THE PARK WERE TWO CIRCLES OF beech trees which enclosed the stables of our Suffolk Punches. The reader should, I suppose, be told that these were a special breed of cart horse, which must originally have been useful, but which by my time were bred almost entirely for their beauty.* They were solid and heavy, but as perfect in proportion as the horses of the Sforzas or the Gonzagas. For ten years the Sudbourne Stud was the most famous in the world and won the first prizes at every show. We all loved them, and visited their stables several times in a week; but the great moment was on Sunday mornings, when they would have coloured ribbons put in their manes and be trotted round to stand for our admiration on the lawn in front of the house. My father would then give them minute peppermints of a brand known as 'Curiously Strong', which made them sneeze, but seemed to give them pleasure. After the ceremony they would trot home to their stables in the beech trees as complacent as Morris dancers. I have often thought that the memory of these dear animals, which I recapture every time I open a 'conker', is the basis of my sense of form. They are, indeed, very clearly connected in my mind with trees, and searching in my mind for the first moments in which I seemed to be lifted out of my immediate childish preoccupations, the first emotions that could be described as religious, they seem to have been inspired by the trunks and roots of trees. Of conventional religious instruction I received nothing at all.

*They are now bred for work, are 17½ hands instead of 15, and have lost the perfect proportions that so much delighted me.

KENNETH CLARK, *from* Another Part of the Wood

3 October – Jos Screams Every Day

HALFWAY THROUGH ORDEAL BY GRANDSON, SEEN BY HIS parents as a period of breaking-in to get the old grey mare accustomed to future duties.

'I scream every day,' Jos says complacently to neighbours who inquire how we're getting on. How right he is. How often we all feel like screaming and how fortunate he is not to have to worry, just go ahead and scream and unload frustrations. And how many frustrations there are. Bringing up children consists almost entirely of imposing more and more, in order, if possible, to turn them from egocentric savages into at least the semblance of a human being. No wonder Jos screams every day, let him scream while he can and make the most of it.

The question of how to deal with Jos is the same, in essence, as the question which currently preoccupies our political leaders, of how to deal with the nation. Basically there are two methods; appeasement and confrontation. Naturally one leans heavily, like Mr Wilson, on appeasement. Jos wakes up early. I mustn't get him up at six o'clock, partly in my own interests and partly in those of his parents, who eschew early rising. On the other hand confrontation at 6 am is uncongenial; and it's all right for Jos to scream every day, but not *all* day.

So this morning I tried a banana: you can have a banana if you go back to bed. Jos agreed to this but of course only for so long as it took him to eat the banana. The social contract was then thrown to the winds. Jos is now around on the upstairs landing. I hear ominous thumps and bangs and he's probably catching a cold, but on the other hand he's still upstairs and isn't actually screaming. So appeasement has more or less worked so far.

But of course there's a limit. Today one banana, tomorrow two bananas? Three? Breakfast in bed? Jos at two-and-a-half has long ago caught on to the principles of blackmail, which follows on appeasement as the night the day. There comes a time when Wilsonian tactics simply must give way to Heathian confrontation. My tone changes from cajolery to a barrack-square bellow. Orders are given. Intimidation is tried. All right,

OVERLEAF:
*Children on a wall,
Ditchear, 1933*

95

kick the door in if you like, it hurts you more than it hurts the door. (I hope: the doors are only made of hollow veneer; once, when we sawed a bit off the bottom of one, we found the inside to be stuffed with egg-cartons.) The screaming becomes demonic and continues unabated for what seems like hours and one hopes it's true that tots don't die of apoplexy.

Confrontation does work if one holds out, but then one has full command of all the resources; Jos can't picket the boiler or dismantle (as yet) the fuse-box. But confrontation is extremely exhausting. It certainly exhausts me more than it exhausts Jos.

ELSPETH HUXLEY, *from* Gallipot Eyes

Tangerine Lanterns

I SAW DIRECTIONS FOR MAKING THESE IN A POPULAR MAGAZINE which cheated by using a night-light. The whole fun and point of making these is that they are night-lights in their own right.

Roll the tangerine between the palms of the hands to loosen the skin, then draw a line with a sharp knife round the hemisphere of the fruit. Gently ease away the skin from the flesh with your thumbs, then take out the flesh segment by segment in order to leave the pith 'core' attached to one half of the skin – this is the wick. When the skin is in two halves, drip candle-wax round and over the wick (trimming it if it is too long). You can use lard, but it doesn't smell as nice. Cut a hole about the size of a 2p piece in the other half of the skin. Light the wick and put the lid on top. Your lantern should last for about 15 minutes at least, and as the top chars a little, the smell is wonderful. We were taught how to make these as children and I've never known a child who wasn't enchanted by these lanterns.

SIMONE SEKERS, *from* Grandmother's Lore

OLD MEMORIES

When shadows stroked the fields, and the earth grew chill
And batlight brought the mice abroad;
When beanfields wove their sweetness down the hill;
When the last rook had cawed:
I, dreaming boy, would leave my bed
And watch the shadows round my head.
    Elm branches pass the moon across the sky,
    A squirrel glides across the lawn; from high
    A wakeful owl invites an answering cry—
    And Memory awakes, and at her sigh
    He lifts his head – oh night! oh thin sad thrill!
    The murmur of the dusty ivy leaves
    Where swallows cling and cherish in the eaves!
    Those wondering boyhood dreams are with me still.

DAVID HODSON

MAGIC

THE WITCHES' CHARM

The owl is abroad, the bat, and the toad,
   And so is the cat-a-mountain;
The ant and the mole sit both in a hole,
   And frog peeps out o'the fountain;
The dogs they do bay, and the timbrels play,
   The spindle is now a-turning;
The moon it is red, and the stars are fled,
   But all the sky is a-burning;
The ditch is made, and our nails the spade,
With pictures full, of wax and of wool;
Their livers I stick with needles quick:
There lacks but the blood to make up the flood.

BEN JONSON

IN THE FARMYARD NEAR THE MIDDLE OF THIS VILLAGE stands, at this day, a row of pollard-ashes, which, by the seams and long cicatrices down their sides, manifestly show that, in former times, they have been cleft asunder. These trees, when young and flexible, were severed and held open by wedges, while ruptured children, stripped naked, were pushed through the apertures, under a persuasion that, by such a process, the poor babes would be cured of their infirmity. As soon as the operation was over, the tree, in the suffering part, was plastered with loam, and carefully swathed up. If the parts coalesced and soldered together, as usually fell out, where the feat was performed with any adroitness at all, the party was cured; but, where the cleft continued to gape, the operation, it was supposed, would prove ineffectual . . . We have several persons now living in the village, who, in their childhood, were supposed to be healed by this superstitious ceremony, derived down perhaps from our Saxon ancestors, who practised it before their conversion to Christianity.

GILBERT WHITE, from Natural History of Selbourne

GLAUCOPIS

John Fane Dingle
  By Rumney Brook
Shot a crop-eared owl,
  For pigeon mistook:

Caught her by the lax wing.
  – She, as she dies,
Thrills his warm soul through
  With her deep eyes.

Corpse-eyes are eerie:
  Tiger-eyes fierce:
John Fane Dingle found
  Owl-eyes worse.

Owl-eyes on night-clouds,
  Constant as Fate:
Owl-eyes in baby's face:
  On dish and plate:

Owl-eyes, without sound.
  – Pale of hue
John died of no complaint,
  With owl-eyes too.

RICHARD HUGHES

AGAINST WENS

Wen, wen, little wen,
Here thou shalt not build, nor have any abode.
But thou must pass forth to the hill hard by,
Where thou hast a brother in misery.
He shall lay a leaf at thy head.

Under the foot of the wolf, under the wing of the eagle,
Under the claw of the eagle, ever mayest thou fade.
Shrivel as coal on the hearth,
Shrink as muck in the wall,
And waste away like water in a bucket.
Become as small as a grain of linseed,
And far smaller also than a hand-worm's hip-bone,
And become even so small that thou become naught.

ANON

*Swimming a witch,
from* Witches
Apprehended,
Examined and
Executed, *1613*

105

5 February 1790

MY POOR COW RATHER BETTER THIS MORNING, BUT NOT able to get up as yet, she having a disorder which I never heard of before or any of our Somerset friends. It is called Tail-shot, that is a separation of some of the Joints of the Tail about a foot from the tip of the Tail, or rather a slipping of one Joint from another. It also makes all her Teeth quite loose in her head. The Cure, is to open that part of the Tail so slipt lengthways and put in an Onion boiled and some salt and bind it up with some coarse Tape.

From the diary of THE REVEREND JAMES WOODFORDE

ON A MIDSUMMER EVE

I idly cut a parsley stalk,
And blew therein towards the moon;
I had not thought what ghosts would walk
With shivering footsteps to my tune.

I went, and knelt, and scooped my hand
As if to drink, into the brook,
And a faint figure seemed to stand
Above me, with the bygone look.

I lipped rough rhymes of chance, not choice,
I thought not what my words might be;
There came into my ear a voice
That turned a tenderer verse for me.

THOMAS HARDY

11 April 1681

I TOOK EARLY IN THE MORNING, GOOD DOSE OF ELIXIR, AND hung three spiders about my neck, and they drove my ague away – *Deo gratias*.

From the diary of ELIAS ASHMOLE

SABRINA'S SONG

By the rushy-fringèd bank,
Where grows the willow and the osier dank,
   My sliding chariot stays,
Thick set with agate, and the azurn sheen
   Of turkis blue, and emerald green,
     That in the channel strays,
   Whilst from off the waters fleet
   Thus I set my printless feet
   O'er the cowslip's velvet head,
     That bends not as I tread.
   Gentle swain, at thy request
     I am here.

JOHN MILTON, *from* Comus

UP ON THE DOWNS

Up on the downs the red-eyed kestrels hover,
Eyeing the grass.
The field-mouse flits like a shadow into cover
As their shadows pass.

Men are burning the gorse on the down's shoulder;
A drift of smoke

OVERLEAF: *The Horn Dance at Abbott's Bromley, Staffs, 1933*

107

Glitters with fire and hangs, and the skies smoulder,
And the lungs choke.

Once the tribe did thus on the downs, on these downs
   burning
Men in the frame.
Crying to the gods of the downs till their brains were
   turning
And the gods came.

And to-day on the downs, in the wind, the hawks, the
   grasses,
In blood and air,
Something passes me and cries as it passes.
On the chalk downland bare.

JOHN MASEFIELD

8 March 1796

OBLIGED TO GET UP IN THE NIGHT AND TAKE SOME mint-water, which instantly relieved me. Must be very careful what I eat: blame pease-soup for this.

From the diary of THE REVEREND W. J. TEMPLE

REMEDY FOR CONSUMPTION

TAKE 20 SNAILS, AND A HANDFUL OF BROAD DAISIES, PUT in a Quart of Water, and gently boil it to a Pint; take a Spoonful every Morning in some Milk.

RICHARD BRADLEY, *1753*

30 April 1870

THIS EVENING BEING MAY EVE I OUGHT TO HAVE PUT SOME birch and wittan (mountain ash) over the door to keep out the 'old witch'. But I was too lazy to go out and get it. Let us hope the old witch will not come in during the night. The young witches are welcome.

From the diary of THE REVEREND FRANCIS KILVERT

AUTUMN

AUTUMN

NOVEMBER

The mellow year is hasting to its close;
The little birds have almost sung their last,
Their small notes twitter in the dreary blast—
That shrill-piped harbinger of early snows;
The patient beauty of the scentless rose,
Oft with the Morn's hoar crystal quaintly glass'd,
Hangs, a pale mourner for the summer past,
And makes a little summer where it grows:
In the chill sunbeam of the faint brief day
The dusky waters shudder as they shine,
The russet leaves obstruct the struggling way
Of oozy brooks, which no deep banks define,
And the gaunt woods, in ragged, scant array,
Wrap their old limbs with sombre ivy twine.

HARTLEY COLERIDGE

THE RIPE AND BEARDED BARLEY

Come out, 'tis now September,
   The hunter's moon's begun,
And through the wheaten stubble
   We hear the frequent gun.
The leaves are turning yellow,
   And fading into red,
While the ripe and bearded barley
   Is hanging down its head.

   All among the barley
     Who would not be blithe,
   While the ripe and bearded barley
     Is smiling on the scythe.

The celebration of
the Harvest Home
c. 1770

The wheat is like a rich man,
    It's sleek and well-to-do,
The oats are like a pack of girls,
    They're thin and dancing, too.
The rye is like a miser,
    Both sulky, lean, and small,
Whilst the ripe and bearded barley
    Is the monarch of them all.

    All among the barley
      Who would not be blithe,
    While the ripe and bearded barley
      Is smiling on the scythe.

The spring is like a young maid
    That does not know her mind,
The summer is a tyrant
    Of most ungracious kind.
The autumn is an old friend
    That pleases all he can,
And brings the bearded barley
    To glad the heart of man.

All among the barley
  Who would not be blithe,
While the ripe and bearded barley
  Is smiling on the scythe.

                                        ANON

NORTH WIND IN OCTOBER

In the golden glade the chestnuts are fallen all;
From the sered boughs of the oak the acorns fall:
The beech scatters her ruddy fire;
The lime hath stripped to the cold,
And standeth naked above her yellow attire:
The larch thinneth her spire
To lay the ways of the wood with cloth of gold.

  Out of the golden-green and white
Of the brake the fir-trees stand upright
In the forest of flame, and wave aloft
To the blue of heaven their blue-green tuftings soft.

But swiftly in shuddering gloom the splendours fail,
As the harrying North-wind beareth
A cloud of skirmishing hail
The grievèd woodland to smite:
In a hurricane through the trees he teareth,
Raking the boughs and the leaves rending,
And whistleth to the descending
Blows of his icy flail.
Gold and snow he mixeth in spite,
And whirleth afar; as away on his winnowing flight
He passeth, and all again for awhile is bright.

                                ROBERT BRIDGES

*Harvesting a
wartime onion crop
in Kent*

FORSAKEN WOODS, TREES WITH SHARP STORMS OPPRESSED

Forsaken woods, trees with sharp storms oppressed,
   Whose leaves once hid the sun, now strew the ground,
   Once bred delight, now scorn, late used to sound
Of sweetest birds, now of hoarse crows the nest;
Gardens, which once in thousand colours dressed
   Showed nature's pride, now in dead sticks abound,
   In whom proud summer's treasure late was found
Now but the rags of winter's torn coat rest;
Meadows whose sides late fair brooks kissed, now slime
   Embraced holds; fields whose youth green and brave
   Promised long life, now frosts lay in the grave:
Say all, and I with them, 'What doth not Time!'
   But they, who knew Time, Time will find again;
   I that fair times lost, on Time call in vain.

ROBERT SIDNEY

118

THE BURNING OF THE LEAVES

Now is the time for the burning of the leaves.
They go to the fire; the nostril pricks with smoke
Wandering slowly into the weeping mist.
Brittle and blotched, ragged and rotten sheaves!
A flame seizes the smouldering ruin, and bites
On stubborn stalks that crackle as they resist.

The last hollyhock's fallen tower is dust:
All the spices of June are a bitter reek,
All the extravagant riches spent and mean.
All burns! the reddest rose is a ghost.
Sparks whirl up, to expire in the mist: the wild
Fingers of fire are making corruption clean.

Now is the time for stripping the spirit bare,
Time for the burning of days ended and done,
Idle solace of things that have gone before,
Rootless hope and fruitless desire are there:
Let them go to the fire with never a look behind.
That world that was ours is a world that is ours no more.

They will come again, the leaf and the flower, to arise
From squalor of rottenness into the old splendour,
And magical scents to a wondering memory bring;
The same glory, to shine upon different eyes.
Earth cares for her own ruins, naught for ours.
Nothing is certain, only the certain spring.

LAURENCE BINYON

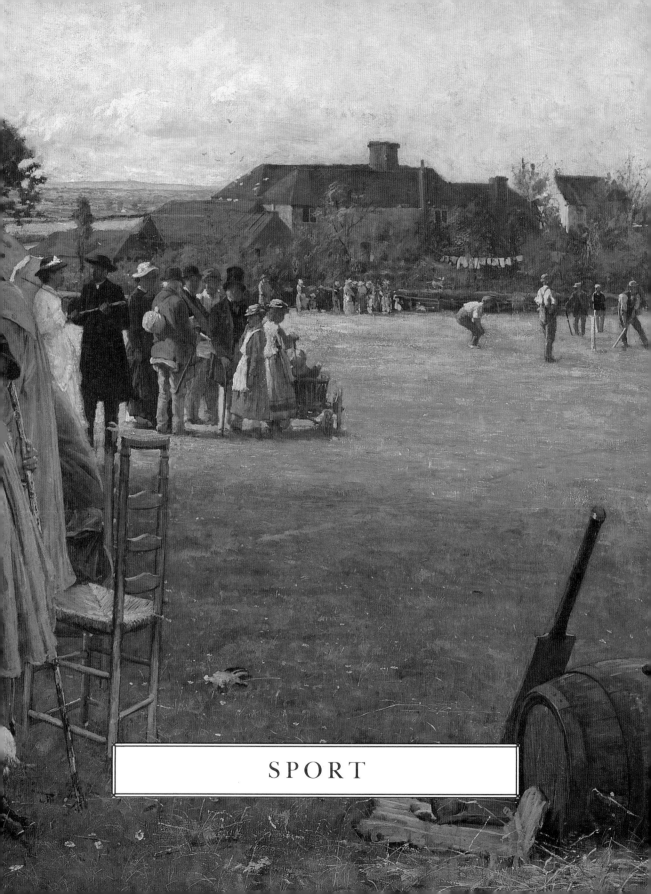

SPORT

1788

I shot a Wood-pecker this Morn in my garden.

From the diary of THE REVEREND JAMES WOODFORDE

15 January 1917

A FEW HOURS IN THE PRE-WAR SURROUNDINGS ...
Pleasant enough; but what a decayed society, hanging
blindly on to the shreds of its traditions. The wet,
watery-green meadows and straggling bare hedges and grey
winding lanes; the cry of hounds, and thud of hoofs, and
people galloping bravely along all around me; and the ride
home with the hounds in the chilly dusk – these are *real* things.
But comfort and respectable squiredom and the futile chatter
of women, and their man-hunting glances, and the pomposity
of port-wine-drinking buffers – what's all that but emptiness?
These people don't reason. They echo one another and their
dead relations, and what they read in papers and dull books.
And they only *see* what they want to see – which is very little
beyond the tips of their red noses. Debrett is on every table;
and heaven a sexless peerage, with a suitable array of depen-
dants and equipages . . .

From the diary of SIEGFRIED SASSOON

June 23rd

TENNIS-PARTY AT WEALTHY AND ELABORATE HOUSE, TO
which Robert and I now bidden for the first time. (Also,
probably, the last.) Immense opulence of host and
hostess at once discernible in fabulous display of deck-chairs,
all of complete stability and miraculous cleanliness. Am

introduced to youngish lady in yellow, and serious young man with horn-rimmed spectacles. Lady in yellow says at once that she is sure I have a lovely garden. (Why?)

Elderly, but efficient-looking, partner is assigned to me, and we play against the horn-rimmed spectacles and agile young creature in expensive crêpe-de-chine. Realise at once that all three play very much better tennis than I do. Still worse, realise that *they* realise this. Just as we begin, my partner observes gravely that he ought to tell me he is a left-handed player. Cannot imagine what he expects me to do about it, lose my head, and reply madly that That is Splendid.

Game proceeds, I serve several double-faults, and elderly partner becomes graver and graver. At beginning of each game he looks at me and repeats score with fearful distinctness, which, as it is never in our favour, entirely unnerves me. At 'Six-*one*' we leave the court and silently seek chairs as far removed from one another as possible. Find myself in vicinity of Our Member, and we talk about the Mace, peeresses in the House of Lords — on which we differ — winter sports, and Alsatian dogs.

Robert plays tennis, and does well.

E. M. DELAFIELD, *from* Diary of a Provincial Lady

SUDDENLY A PHEASANT IS HURLED OUT OF A NEIGHBOURING copse; something crosses the road; and out over a large and shining meadow goes a fox, tall and red, going easily as if he sailed in the wind. He crosses that meadow, then another, and he is half a mile away before a loud halloo sounds in the third field, and a mile away before the first hound crosses the road upon his scent.

Run hard, hounds, and drown the jackdaws' calling with your concerted voices. It is good to see your long swift train across the meadow and away, away; on such a day a man would give everything to run like that. Run hard, fox, and may you escape, for it would not be well to die on such a day, unless you

Shooting Flying,
from The
Gentleman's
Recreation *by*
Richard Blome,
1686

could perchance first set your fair teeth into the throats of the foolish ones who now break through the hedge on great horses and pursue you – I know not why – ignorant of the command that has gone forth from the heart of this high blue heaven, Be beautiful and enjoy and live!

EDWARD THOMAS, *from* The Heart of England

AS FOR HIMSELF, HE WOULD TAKE THE LOWER REACHES: and, with this fine gesture of self-sacrifice, Mr Stephenson left me to assemble my rod, select my bait and get on with the business of the day which, according to himself, must be never allowed to become a business at all. And I am sure that had he returned to watch my progress, Mr Stephenson would not have been disappointed at the way I was behaving, for, having got my rod together – and it was far too weighty a rod for a small boy like myself – I lay down on the bank, the better to digest the chicken and all the other good things.

I watched the dragonflies and I remember seeing the lazy fish lurking in the shadows: and, once or twice, the thin line of bubbles that showed an otter was swimming under water. I noticed, too, that the fish which, I should have thought, would have panicked at the presence of the otter, did no such thing. They simply froze. Even their tails, which had, up to now, been moving gently from side to side, stopped altogether, until, from their beginning to move again, I guessed the otter had passed.

Sure enough, she had: for, as I lay there so silently watching, I saw the dark, sleek, almost black body, dripping with water, come out on the far bank of the river and, for a moment, she stood there, long and low on the ground, with the water dripping off her and the sun lighting up her dark body, so that it sparkled like diamonds, until, across the meadow, in little dashes and then freezing quite still, another otter – much smaller – came to join her.

It was charming. It was very beautiful, as the two otters, their

lips drawn back as though they were laughing, began gambol-
ling and playing on the river bank. They chased each other
backwards and forwards. They leapt over each other and gave
each other playful little nips. They – in that summer afternoon
on the river bank – had not a care in the world, while the little
boy watched and the fish slept and the grey horse – when I
could see him from the corner of my eye – grazed on the lush
grass.

And then, in a moment, there was a fearful splash and an
inhuman stuttering yell and the otters had gone as though they
had never been there and the fish had fled and the grey horse
had his ears pricked.

I jumped up.

I looked for Mr Stephenson: but he was not where we had
had lunch. There was no sign of him on the bank. What had
been the splash then and why had the otters fled and the fish
disappeared and the horse had his ears cocked?

It was then that I saw him, struggling in the water and he
gave then another of those stuttering cries. Even as I saw him,
Mr Stephenson managed to struggle to his feet and the fear I
had felt that he might be drowned was dispelled, for I saw the
water came no higher than his middle. But, for all that, he
continued to shout for assistance, and I ran to help him, though
there was little a boy of my size could do to get him out of the
water.

When I reached the bank opposite him, Mr Stephenson was
groping at the roots of the trees, trying to find a way to pull
himself out, but he never had much success for he could only
use one hand, as, in the other, he was still clutching the now
half empty bottle of whisky.

In the end – but I don't remember how – he did get out of
the stream and lay down with the greatest good nature in the
sun to dry his clothes.

From time to time he took a swig at the whisky and his spirits
returned as he pledged me to secrecy, for, said he, it would
never do if Mrs Stephenson knew he had fallen in the river. She
would be worried to death that he caught a cold.

Cold, he repeated, and, indicating the bottle, assured me it was the finest thing in the world to keep out a cold.

It was evening before the whisky was finished and Mr Stephenson's clothes were sufficiently dry for us to go home.

But, by that time, the grey horse had given us up as hopeless and had disappeared. We stood on the side of the road, hopeless and disconsolate, and were very lucky when a farmer driving into Hadleigh gave us a lift.

Mr Stephenson promised he would collect the rods and baskets the next day: but I was not to say that, in case I was misunderstood.

I didn't.

SIMON DEWES, *from* A Suffolk Childhood

23 June 1906

LEFT OFF STRAW HAT. TOO HEAVY.
Although Vice-Captain, I am left out of cricket team. They lost disgracefully. By the by, I saw a fellow get killed while batting. Bit of a damper. Shadows before my eyes. I wonder what is the reason for it.

From the diary of SYDNEY MOSELEY

CHARLES PLAYED CRICKET. 'I EXPECT YOU HAD A SLAP-UP tea,' I remarked on his return; Oaksey had been playing the Royal Agricultural College, one of their grander fixtures. Everyone supposes the students to be rich and upper-class, with fast cars and glamorous girl-friends. 'No, it was bloody awful,' he said. 'Thick slabs of dry bread, a bare scrape of butter and half a jar of seedy pips going by the name of raspberry jam.' Disappointing. 'If my missus gave me a tea like that I'd throw her over the allotments,' one of the Oaksey team had remarked. 'These posh people don't eat half as well as we do,' said another. 'My dad used to work for the Whosis and said he'd be ashamed to sit down in our kitchen to what they had for dinner. Bloody great Rover in the garage, he said, and left-over scrag-end in the fridge.'

Catharine does the Oaksey teas in our village hall and they're excellent. 'Nice thin-cut sandwiches, two or three kinds, cucumbers and tomatoes as well as jam,' Charles observed. The Oaksey XI preened themselves not only on their teas but on their prowess: much to their surprise, they won the game.

ELSPETH HUXLEY, *from* Gallipot Eyes

31 January 1823

A WET DAY, AND AS NO JACKANAPES COULD GET HIS GUN off in the rain it was my only chance; I therefore sallied out for one huge swan that had been the target of the coast, and had become so wild that he could scarcely be looked

The rabbit trapper, 1948

at: on my way out I fired a long shot and got 4 geese; soon after, as I expected, we saw this huge bird, floating about in a rough sea, and in a pour of rain; I had two punts to manoeuvre on one side of him, while Reade and I drifted down on the other; he sprung at about four hundred yards, came luckily across my punt at about 75 yards, and down I fetched him, like a cock pheasant, with the swivel gun. His fall was more like the parachute of an air balloon than a bird; he was shot quite dead; he weighed 21 lb, and measured 7 feet 8 inches from wing to wing, being the largest, by far, of any I had killed; therefore my misfortune of last night was balanced by getting another wild swan.

From the diary of COLONEL PETER HAWKER

THE FOLLOWING DAY YOU WILL PROBABLY BE AWAKENED BY angry voices in the hall beneath your room. Pay no attention to these but quickly go to sleep again. It is a curious anomaly that, while most men pretend to like shooting, it invariably brings their worst passions to the surface, especially when they are getting ready to leave the house after breakfast. If you wish to be really tactful, stay in bed until quite twelve o'clock. No hostess wants to be bothered with her women guests in the morning unless there are some men about to amuse them. Above all, remember that you will probably be obliged to go out to lunch with the guns and spend the afternoon with them, so put on your stoutest tweeds (choosing a colour that will not shock the birds), thick shoes, and a mackintosh.

On arriving at the appointed place for lunch, which will be either, if you are lucky, a warm room in some cottage, or, more probably, a windswept haystack, you will certainly have to wait for at least an hour. This time is occupied in unpacking the lunch and gossiping. When at last the men appear, do not speak to them until they have addressed you first. If the shooting has been good they will come up to you smiling, saying something like 'Well, well, this isn't the worst part of the day is it, what? Ha, ha, what?' and conversation will then flow smoothly and cheerfully. If it has been bad, on the other hand, the tactful woman remains silent until the softening influence of food and drink has been felt.

After luncheon you will accompany the guns to some bleak hedgerow, where you will sit quite still for a great time, preferably in silence. If, however, you must speak, be careful at all costs to avoid remarks like 'Please don't beat poor Fido quite so hard,' or 'Oh, would you mind killing off that wounded hare? It reminds me of Aunt Florence.'

When the man with whom you are standing breaks a heavy silence by saying angrily, 'Shut up and lie down,' remember that he is most probably addressing not you, but his dog.

NANCY MITFORD, *in* Vogue, *11 December 1929*

THE FIRST BIRD I SEARCHED FOR WAS THE NIGHTJAR, which used to nest in the valley. Its song is like the sound of a stream of wine spilling from a height into a deep and booming cask. It is an odorous sound, with a bouquet that rises to the quiet sky. In the glare of day it would seem thinner and drier, but dusk mellows it and gives it vintage. If a song could smell, this song would smell of crushed grapes and almonds and dark wood. The sound spills out, and none of it is lost. The whole wood brims with it. Then it stops. Suddenly, unexpectedly. But the ear hears it still, a prolonged and fading echo, draining and winding out among the surrounding trees.

J. A. BAKER, *from* The Peregrine

HOME LIFE

HAVING PASSED THE RUINED ABBEY AND THE ORCHARD, I came to a long, low farmhouse kitchen, smelling of bacon and herbs and burning sycamore and ash. A gun, a blunderbuss, a pair of silver spurs, and a golden spray of last year's corn hung over the high mantelpiece and its many brass candlesticks; and beneath was an open fireplace and a perpetual red fire, and two teapots warming, for they had tea for breakfast, tea for dinner, tea for tea, tea for supper, and tea between. The floor was of sanded slate flags, and on them a long many-legged table, an oak settle, a table piano, and some Chippendale chairs. There were also two tall clocks; and they were the most human clocks I ever met, for they ticked with effort and uneasiness: they seemed to think and sorrow over time, as if they caused it, and did not go on thoughtlessly or impudently like most clocks, which are insufferable; they found the hours troublesome and did not twitter mechanically over them; and at midnight the twelve strokes always nearly ruined them, so great was the effort. On the wall were a large portrait of Spurgeon, several sets of verses printed and framed in memory of dead members of the family, an allegorical tree watered by the devil, and photographs of a bard and of Mr Lloyd George. There were about fifty well-used books near the fire, and two or three men smoking, and one man reading some serious book aloud, by the only lamp; and a white girl was carrying out the week's baking, of large loaves, flat fruit tarts of blackberry, apple, and whinberry, plain golden cakes, large soft currant biscuits, and curled oat cakes. And outside, the noises of a west wind and a flooded stream, the whimper of an otter, and the long, slow laugh of an owl.

EDWARD THOMAS, *from* A Farmhouse

HOWEVER UNWORKMANLIKE THE DEED, IT HAD BEEN mercifully done. The blood flowed out in a torrent instead of in the trickling stream she had desired. The dying animal's cry assumed its third and final tone, the shriek of agony; his glazing eyes riveting themselves on Arabella with the eloquently keen reproach of a creature recognizing at last the treachery of those who had seemed his only friends.

'Make un stop that!' said Arabella. 'Such a noise will bring somebody or other up here, and I don't want people to know we are doing it ourselves.' Picking up the knife from the ground whereon Jude had flung it, she slipped it into the gash, and slit the windpipe. The pig was instantly silent, his dying breath coming through the hole.

'That's better,' she said.

'It is a hateful business!' said he.

'Pigs must be killed.'

The animal heaved in a final convulsion, and, despite the rope, kicked out with all his last strength. A tablespoonful of black clot came forth, the trickling of red blood having ceased for some seconds.

'That's it; now he'll go,' said she. 'Artful creatures – they always keep back a drop like that as long as they can!'

The last plunge had come so unexpectedly as to make Jude stagger, and in recovering himself he kicked over the vessel in which the blood had been caught.

'There!' she cried, thoroughly in a passion. 'Now I can't make any blackpot. There's a waste, all through you!'

Jude put the pail upright, but only about a third of the whole steaming liquid was left in it, the main part being splashed over the snow, and forming a dismal, sordid, ugly spectacle – to those who saw it as other than an ordinary obtaining of meat. The lips and nostrils of the animal turned livid, then white, and the muscles of his limbs relaxed.

'Thank God!' Jude said. 'He's dead.'

'What's God got to do with such a messy job as a pig-killing, I should like to know!' she said scornfully. 'Poor folks must live.'

THOMAS HARDY, *from* Jude the Obscure

OPPOSITE: *Scene from an angora rabbit farm, Gloucestershire, 1935*

ODAY HAV JOHN AND I BIN WED THIS 3 YERE AND HERE I do set down all that I do every day.

Today I did do my butter maken, leving Sarah to cook most of the dinner, as the butter was longe time cummin, indeed not till John had put in a crown piece and turned did it cum. Sarah did burne the dinner, like she always do, and John was very cross therebye, he mislyking Sarahs cooken, so I do sometimes hav to let him think it is me. Men be verry tiresome sometimes.

ANNE HUGHES, *from* Diary of a Farmer's Wife

AFTERNOON WORKS

Make company break,
Go cherish the weak.

When dinner is ended, set servants to work,
and follow such fellows as loveth to lurk.

To servant in sicknesse see nothing ye grutch,
a thing of a trifle shall comfort him much.

Who many do feed,
Save much they had need.

Put chippings in dippings, use parings to save,
fat capons or chickens that lookest to have.

Save droppings and skimmings, how ever ye do,
for medicine for cattle, for cart and for shoe.

Lean capon unmeet,
Dear fed is unsweet.

Such offcorn as cometh give wife to her fee,
feed willingly such as do help to feed thee

138

Though fat fed is dainty, yet this I thee warn,
be cunning in fatting for robbing thy barn.

Piece hole to defend.
Things timely amend.

Good sempsters be sewing of fine pretty knacks,
good huswifes be mending and piecing their sacks.

Though making and mending be huswifely ways,
yet mending in time is the huswife to praise.

Buy new as is meet,
Mark blanket and sheet.

Though ladies may rend and buy new ery day,
good huswifes must mend and buy new as they may.

Call quarterly servants to court and to leet,
write every coverlet, blanket, and sheet.

Save feathers for guest,
These other rob chest.

Save wing for a thresher, when gander doth die,
save feather of all thing, the softer to lie.

Much spice is a thief, so is candle and fire,
sweet sauce is as crafty as ever was friar.

Wife make thine owne candle,
Spare penny to handle.

Provide for thy tallow, ere frost cometh in,
and make thine owne candle, ere winter begin.
THOMAS TUSSER, *from* Hundreth Good Pointes of Husbandrie

6 April 1961

I AM VERY HAPPY THESE SPRING DAYS. EACH MORNING I WAKE between 4 a.m. and 5 a.m.; then make tea, read for a while, work until 7.30, when I go for a walk. Through the window I watch the day begin, from first grey light to full sunrise, as, in the evening, I watch it end. It is a great joy to see each day's first and last light. After breakfast I read the papers, then work until lunch time. After lunch, I lie down with a book, and usually sleep for an hour or so; then walk or do gardening, mostly mowing the grass; followed by a late tea, work until about 7.30, another short stroll, supper, a game of cards with Kitty, and bed. This quiet and serenity set one apart from public affairs. The newspapers, which I still avidly devour, seem to be about another world than mine. I continue to want to know about it, but not to visit it.

A paperback series of religious books has, for its first volume, St Augustine's *Confessions*, and for its second *Sex, Love and Marriage*. In contemporary terms, anything about fornication is religious, as anything about raising the standard of life, and ameliorating its material circumstances, is Christian. In this sense fornication can be seen as sacred, an act of Holy Communion – which, as Euclid says, is absurd.

From the diary of MALCOLM MUGGERIDGE

B UT IT WAS FROM ONE LITTLE WINDOW, WITH ITS BLIND drawn down, a mere blank transparency on the night, that the sense of home and the little curtained world within walls – the larger stressful world of outside Nature shut out and forgotten – most pulsated. Close against the white blind hung a bird-cage, clearly silhouetted, every wire, perch, and appurtenance distinct and recognizable, even to yesterday's dull-edged lump of sugar. On the middle perch the fluffy occupant, head tucked well into feathers, seemed so near to them as to be easily stroked, had they tried; even the delicate tips of his plumped-out plumage pencilled plainly on the illuminated screen. As they looked, the sleepy little fellow stirred uneasily, woke, shook himself, and raised his head. They could see the gape of his tiny beak as he yawned in a bored sort of way, looked round, and then settled his head into his back again, while the ruffled feathers gradually subsided into perfect stillness. Then a gust of bitter wind took them in the back of the neck, a small sting of frozen sleet on the skin woke them as from a dream, and they knew their toes to be cold and their legs tired, and their own home distant a weary way . . .

They plodded along steadily and silently, each of them thinking his own thoughts. The Mole's ran a good deal on supper, as it was pitch dark, and it was all a strange country to him as far as he knew, and he was following obediently in the wake of the Rat, leaving the guidance entirely to him. As for the Rat, he was walking a little way ahead, as his habit was, his shoulders humped, his eyes fixed on the straight grey road in front of him; so he did not notice poor Mole when suddenly the summons reached him, and took him like an electric shock.

We others, who have long lost the more subtle of the physical senses, have not even proper terms to express an animal's intercommunications with his surroundings, living or otherwise, and have only the word 'smell', for instance, to include the whole range of delicate thrills which murmur in the nose of the animal night and day, summoning, warning, inciting, repelling. It was one of these mysterious fairy calls from out the void that suddenly reached Mole in the darkness, making him tingle through and through with its very familiar appeal, even while as yet he could not clearly remember what it was. He stopped dead in his tracks, his nose searching hither and thither in its efforts to recapture the fine filament, the telegraphic current, that had so strongly moved him. A moment, and he had caught it again; and with it this time came recollection in fullest flood.

Home! That was what they meant, those caressing appeals, those soft touches wafted through the air, those invisible little hands pulling and tugging, all one way! Why, it must be quite close by him at that moment, his old home that he had

hurriedly forsaken and never sought again, that day when he
first found the river! And now it was sending out its scouts and
its messengers to capture him and bring him in. Since his
escape on that bright morning he had hardly given it a thought,
so absorbed had he been in his new life, in all its pleasures, its
surprises, its fresh and captivating experiences. Now, with a
rush of old memories, how clearly it stood up before him, in the
darkness! Shabby indeed, and small and poorly furnished, and
yet his, the home he had made for himself, the home he had
been so happy to get back to after his day's work. And the home
had been happy with him, too, evidently, and was missing him,
and wanted him back, and was telling him so, through his nose,
sorrowfully, reproachfully, but with no bitterness or anger;
only with plaintive reminder that it was there, and wanted him.

KENNETH GRAHAME, *from* The Wind in the Willows

A Gammon of Badger Roasted

THE BADGER IS ONE OF THE CLEANEST CREATURES IN ITS
Food of any in the World; and one may suppose that
the Flesh of this Creature is not unwholesome. It eats
like the finest Pork, but much sweeter.

Lay the Gammon in a Brine of Salt, and Water that will bear
an Egg, for a Week or ten Days, then boil it till it is tender, and

after roast it, strewing it with Flour and rasped Bread sifted, in the manner of a Westphalian Ham. Serve it hot with a Garnish of Bacon fried in Cutlets, and some Lemon in Slices.

RICHARD BRADLEY, *1753*

LINES FOR A BED AT KELMSCOTT MANOR

The wind's on the wold
And the night is a-cold,
And Thames runs chill
'Twixt mead and hill,
But kind and dear
Is the old house here,
And my heart is warm
Midst winter's harm.
Rest then and rest,
And think of the best
'Twixt summer and spring
When all birds sing
In the town of the tree,
And ye lie in me
And scarce dare move
Lest earth and its love
Should fade away
Ere the full of the day.

I am old and have seen
Many things that have been,
Both grief and peace,
And wane and increase.
No tale I tell
Of ill or well,
But this I say,
Night treadeth on day,

And for worst and best
Right good is rest.

WILLIAM MORRIS

AN ANCIENT COUNTRY SEAT

YOU MUST EXPECT NOTHING REGULAR IN MY DESCRIPTION of a house that seems to be built before rules were in fashion; the whole is so disjointed and the parts so detached from each other and yet so joining again one cannot tell how, that (in a poetical fit) you would imagine it had been a village in Amphion's time, where twenty cottages had taken a dance together, were all out, and stood still in amazement ever since. A stranger would be grievously disappointed who should ever think to get into this house the right way; one would expect after entering through the porch to be let into the hall; alas! nothing less; you find yourself in a brewhouse. From the parlour you think to step into the drawing-room; but upon opening the iron-nailed door, you are convinced by a flight of birds about your ears, and a cloud of dust in your eyes, that it is the pigeon-house. On each side our porch are two chimneys, that wear their greens on the outside, which would do as well within, for whenever we make a fire, we let the smoke out of the windows. Over the parlour window hangs a sloping balcony, which time has turned to a very convenient pent-house. The top is crowned with a very venerable tower, so like that of the church just by, that the jackdaws build in it as if it were the true steeple.

ALEXANDER POPE

IN THE COUNTRY A GOOD STORE-ROOM IS SO INDISPENSABLE that where there is none it ought to be built; it should be on the same floor with, and as near as possible to, the kitchen, and, as this would be on the ground floor, it would be necessary to make a cellar underneath, or to raise the building a little distance from the ground, to prevent its being damp, above all things to be guarded against, in a place where stores are kept. It may, perhaps, be kept dry by flues, from the kitchen fire; and this would be a saving of fuel and labour; but if not practicable, the room should have a fire place . . . For bottles of green gooseberries, peas, or any kind of fruit preserved dry, without sugar, have shelves with holes in them, to turn the bottles with their necks downwards. This effectually excludes the air.

ANNE COBBETT, *from* The English Housekeeper

'. . . In my garden ground,
Let still the esculents abound;
Let first the onion flourish there,
Rose among roots, the maiden fair;
Wine-scented and poetic soul
Of the capacious salad bowl.
Let thyme the mountaineer (to dress
The tinier birds) and wading cress,
The lover of the shallow brook
From all my plots and borders look.

Nor crisp and ruddy radish, nor
Pease-cods for the child's pinafore
Be lacking; nor of salad clan
The last and least that ever ran
About great nature's garden beds.
Nor thence be missed the speary heads
Of artichoke, nor thence the bean
That, gathered innocent and green
Outsavours the belauded pea.'

ANON

145

I HAVE FOUND ONE THING TO THANK THIS WET SUMMER FOR. I have never known the conditions so ideal for getting up dandelions. They come up as affably as carrots, one would think it was their vocation. I lay them on the path in rows, patriarchal mandrake rooted specimens, long tapering specimens in their prime of dandelion-hood, and even those poor skinny little infants that hide under blue primroses & pretend to be blue primroses themselves.

Of course if I thought that next year there would be no dandelions at all, I should be very sorry. But I don't doubt there will be quite enough left to give me that particular pleasure of the dandelions that appear like defiant ancient Britons and have the first pure honey-scent of the year.

The day before yesterday, I appeased a life-long ambition: I held a young fox in my arms. He was an orphan – in other words, the vixen had been killed – a small rickety orphan, when he was given to Mrs Cox six months ago. Now he is the elegant young friend of the family; gentler than a dog, more demonstrative than a cat. I held him in my arms, & snuffed his wild geranium smell, and suddenly he thrust his long nose under my chin, and burrowed against my shoulder, and subsided into bliss. His paws are very soft, soft as raspberries. Everything about him is elegant – an Adonis of an animal. His profile is intensely sophisticated, his full face is the image of artless candour. His fur is like rather coarse, very thick, swansdown, & he wears a grey stomacher.

Heavens . . .

SYLVIA TOWNSEND WARNER, *letter to George Plank, 4 September 1958*

6 May 1870

AS I ENTERED THE FOLD OF GILFACH Y RHEOL, JANET ISSUED from the house door and rushed across the yard and turning the corner of the wain-house I found the two younger ladies assisting at the castration of the lambs, catching and holding the poor little beasts and standing by whilst the operation was performed, seeming to enjoy the spectacle. It was the first time I had seen clergyman's daughters helping to castrate lambs or witnessing that operation and it rather gave me a turn of disgust at first.

From the diary of THE REVEREND FRANCIS KILVERT

EXTRACT FROM BLUE REMEMBERED HILLS

Into my heart an air that kills
  From yon far country blows:
What are those blue remembered hills,
  What spires, what farms are those?

That is the land of lost content,
  I see it shining plain,
The happy highways where I went
  And cannot come again.

A. E. HOUSMAN

OTHER PEOPLE

DEAR SIR,

I am in a madhouse & quite forget your name or who you are
you must excuse me for I have nothing to commu[n]icate or tell
of & why I am shut up I dont know I have nothing to say so I
conclude

yours respectfully John Clare
Mr J. Hipkins

JOHN CLARE, letter to James Hipkins, 8 March 1860

TWO FROGS I MET IN EARLY CHILDHOOD HAVE LINGERED IN
my memory: I frightened one frog, and the other frog
frightened me.

The frightened frog evinced fear by placing its two hands on
its head: at least, I have since understood that a frog assumes
this attitude when in danger, and my frog assumed it.

The alarming frog startled me, 'gave me quite a turn,' as
people say, by jumping when I did not know it was near me . . .

But seeing that matters are as they are – because frogs and
suchlike cannot in reason frighten us now – is it quite certain
that no day will ever come when even the smallest, weakest,
most grotesque, *wronged* creature will not in some fashion rise
up in the Judgemnt with us to condemn us, and so frighten us
effactually once for all?

CHRISTINA ROSSETTI, from Time Flies

22 July 1871

MRS NOTT TOLD ME THAT LOUIE OF THE CLOGGAU WAS
staying in Presteign with her aunt Miss Sylvester, the
woman frog. This extraordinary being is partly a
woman and partly a frog. Her head and face, her eyes and

mouth are those of a frog, and she has a frog's legs and feet. She cannot walk but she hops. She wears very long dresses to cover and conceal her feet which are shod with something like a cow's hoof. She never goes out except to the Primitive Methodist Chapel. Mrs Nott said she had seen this person's frog feet and had seen her in Presteign hopping to and from the Chapel exactly like a frog. She had never seen her hands. She is a very good person. The story about this unfortunate being is as follows. Shortly before she was born a woman came begging to her mother's door with two or three little children. Her mother was angry and ordered the woman away. 'Get away with your young frogs,' she said. And the child she was expecting was born partly in the form of a frog, as a punishment and a curse upon her.

From the diary of THE REVEREND FRANCIS KILVERT

THE HILL FARMER SPEAKS

I am the farmer, stripped of love
And thought and grace by the land's hardness;
But what I am saying over the fields'
Desolate acres, rough with dew,
Is, Listen, listen, I am a man like you.

The wind goes over the hill pastures
Year after year, and the ewes starve,
Milkless, for want of the new grass.
And I starve, too, for something the spring
Can never foster in veins run dry.

The pig is a friend, the cattle's breath
Mingles with mine in the still lanes;
I wear it willingly like a cloak
To shelter me from your curious gaze.

The hens go in and out at the door
From sun to shadow, as stray thoughts pass
Over the floor of my wide skull.
The dirt is under my cracked nails;
The tale of my life is smirched with dung;
The phlegm rattles. But what I am saying
Over the grasses rough with dew
Is, Listen, listen, I am a man like you.

R. S. THOMAS

DUMMY WAS A MAN OF, I SUPPOSE, THIRTY TO FORTY, WHEN I was a child of about eight or nine. He had been a deaf-mute from birth. He lived at the top of Angel Street with his widowed mother in a tiny little cottage that was, I remember, scrupulously clean . . .

He was all right at home, but nobody could keep Dummy at home all the time. He was young. He was strong. He could not read or write, but he could stand on street corners and watch the world go by and, in his dim brain, he must, I think, have been able to appreciate things like the swallows who gathered on the telephone wires before their migration and the excitement of market-days when he could see movement all around him and he must have been able to enjoy the warmth of the sun. He was short and stocky and had a full reddish brown beard and his face was a mass of scars, for, in those days, all our roads were of untarred granite or gravel and it was the easiest thing in the world for Dummy's tormentors to pick up a stone at their feet and hurl it at that bearded figure that stood motionless on the corner.

No sooner, of course, had one stone been thrown than all the other louts in the area began to pelt them at this wretched creature who, as the granite and stones cut into his unprotected flesh, uttered the most horrible and heart-rending shrieks and wails which were all that his wretched vocal organs could produce . . .

No sooner did the dreadful sounds start than the hail of stones and pieces of granite grew stronger and faster, until Dummy's face was streaming with blood and his beard was clotted with it, and, still making those animal sounds, he fled, as though he were, indeed, some hunted animal, and hid in any backyard he could find.

For years this had been the best fun to be had in Hadleigh ... and, time and again, my father was sent for to bandage and get grit out of wounds and generally patch up. But, apart from this, my father did absolutely nothing and I have never been able to understand his attitude.

He was a just and good man. I do not think he had a great deal of imagination: or, if he heeded it in his youth, he had rigorously schooled it out of himself when he was young. He had himself suffered both physically and emotionally, but, as I remember him (he was fifty when I was born and I was thirty-eight when he died), he never showed any emotion at all.

To me, as a child, the sight of Dummy, blood streaming from his wounds, those unearthly sounds coming from his wretched mouth, was such a shock and horror that it has remained with me all through life, so that, for years, I would awake in the middle of the night, screaming as though the louts of Hadleigh were pursuing me.

SIMON DEWES, *from* A Suffolk Childhood

OLD SHEPHERD'S PRAYER

Up to the bed by the window, where I be lyin',
Comes bells and bleat of the flock wi' they two children's clack.
Over, from under the eaves there's the starlings flyin',
And down in yard, fit to burst his chain, yapping out at Sue I do hear
   young Mac.

Turning around like a falled-over sack
I can see team ploughin' in Whithy-bush field and meal carts
    startin' up road to Church-Town;
Saturday arternoon the men goin' back
And the women from market, trapin' home over the down.

Heavenly Master, I wud like to wake to they same green places
Where I be know'd for breakin' dogs and follerin' sheep.
And if I may not walk in th' old ways and look on th' old faces
I wud sooner sleep.

CHARLOTTE MEW

AS I WAS YESTERDAY MORNING WALKING WITH SIR ROGER before his House, a Country-Fellow brought him a huge Fish, which, he told him, Mr *William Wimble* had caught that very Morning; and that he presented it, with his Service, to him, and intended to come and dine with him. At the same Time he delivered a Letter, which my Friend read to me as soon as the Messenger left him.

    '*Sir* Roger,

    I Desire you to accept of a Jack, which is the best I have caught this Season. I intend to come and stay with you a Week, and see how the Perch bite in the *Black River*. I observed, with some Concern, the last Time I saw you upon the Bowling-Green, that your Whip wanted a Lash to it: I will bring half a Dozen with me that I twisted last Week, which I hope will serve you all the Time you are in the Country. I have not been out of the Saddle for six Days last past, having been at *Eaton* with Sir *John*'s eldest Son. He takes to his Learning hugely. I am,

SIR, Your humble Servant,
Will. Wimble.'

JOSEPH ADDISON, *in* The Spectator, *No. 108*

I SUPPOSE THE POOR SOUL WAS ABOUT FIVE OR SIX AND twenty. All she had upon her was a tattered straw bonnet, actual fritters of a petticoat, a very ragged cloth waistcoat with long sleeves, a few strips of cloth which had once been an apron; no linen, gown, shoes, stockings, cap or handkerchief!

She said how thankful she should be to make herself clean and desired that nobody might come to her for some time as she should wash herself completely. Before this, when she was in the kitchen, she begged that none of us should come near her, for that she had the torments of the earth upon her [meaning vermin] . . . When dressed the poor woman went to take up her child who had been lying on the ground and the poor little thing at first cryed bitterly from not knowing her in her altered attire; this delighted the poor mother exceedingly and she was full of it afterwards both here and in the village.

She sat down again to put on a little skirt and coloured frock that Betty had parted with to the poor infant, who had none; and whose naked little cold arms had made Betty cry bitterly, pressing at the same time her own sweet child closely to her as if to guard her from such wretchedness. As the poor woman was dressing her child she stopt every now and then as if to collect her thoughts and said in a tranquil tone of voice 'How light my heart feels! Now I am fit to die! I am clean and comfortable; before I was so dirty the Lord could not receive me' . . .

From the diary of PENELOPE HIND

. . . This is the time of year when we used to see gipsies. They had a regular pitch near by, which they used in their regular yearly round between wintering in the New Forest & summering on Sedgemoor. But the bushes have been grubbed up & a bungalow built, and they come no longer. I miss them – their grave brown faces & their low voices and their stately attitudes as they sat down on the doorstep. There was the grandmother with her grizzled hair in six tight pigtails, and Georgina with a new baby every year, the image of Madonna-like motherhood, who knocked out a policeman with one blow.

The strangest and loveliest sight I ever had of them was in Dorchester: a young girl, an imported bride (if you make a grand match, the bride is imported from the Balkans, where the stock is exceptionally pure and pedigreed). She was being taken shopping by a crone of a duenna who was instructing her, in Romany. I suppose she was about sixteen, very slender, very modest. She wore a full skirt of the brightest circus-pink gingham and a scarlet bodice, & her smooth thin arms wore heavy silver bracelets, and her narrow feet were in plimsoles. Then they went into the grocery-shop (one of the few first-rate shops in Dorchester). Later, I asked my friend across the counter what they had bought. Tea, he said. All the gipsies buy their tea from us. They are very particular, they buy our best tea. The thing that made the deepest impression on me, even

Gipsy family with traditional horse-drawn bow-top van

157

deeper than the girl's beauty, was her aristocratic aloofness. The circus-pink & scarlet & the bracelets naturally aroused attention: people stopped to stare at her. She was as unconcerned, as remote, as though she came from another world.

SYLVIA TOWNSEND WARNER, *letter to Emily Maxwell, 11 February 1975*

9 April 1943

THIS EVENING I SAW A WHITE BICYCLE; AND WHENEVER I see a white bicycle it spells madness to me, for when I was small the doctor's wife in our village was mad, and she rode a white bicycle.

Dressed in her mauve riding-habit and her thick veil she could be seen all over the village, riding her white bicycle, pouring milk down the drains (to feed the German prisoners confined down there), carrying her badminton racket, going round to each house in an attempt to get people to join her badminton club.

Once, my aunt told me, she was discovered directing the traffic dressed in football boots and shorts.

The poor doctor also had his Sunday joint thoroughly washed under the tap, to get rid of the poison.

Often the doctor's wife slept in a barn in the hay, but at other times she would go home and sleep in her room as she used to do.

It was after the last war that she finally went mad. My aunt said that she had always been a little eccentric.

I remembered wondering, even as a child, how it was that she was left entirely to roam freely.

'But mightn't she do something dangerous? Mightn't she hurt herself?' I asked.

'The doctor says that it is much kinder to let her lead the kind of life she likes. She doesn't do anyone any harm,' my aunt answered.

I think she and the doctor were right, although it is obvious to me now that the reason for leaving the mad woman unmolested was an economic one.

She really seemed to lead a vital life, however fantastic and ridiculous she made herself. Shut up in a home, or with a keeper, she could not direct the traffic, could not be of heroic service to poor imprisoned aliens, could not organize thrilling badminton clubs, sleep in the hay, wear mauve riding-habits, decontaminate the Sunday joint, ride on her romantic white bicycle over the common in the evening, talking and singing to herself mysterious and important words.

Oh, how my heart bled for her! I thought of her alone in the hay – the whole wreck of her life – the fiendish laughter of the village children who were worse than devils.

It was shaming, utterly shaming to think that no one cared what she did; that no one would ever take anything she did seriously.

From the diary of DENTON WELCH

7 March 1818

GET ON BUT SLOWLY WITH BEDE AND HERE I HAVE TO record the loss of an old and faithful friend in my little dog Pam who was unfortunately killed by my son's horse laying upon him in the stable where he was sent to dry himself after having been washed and was forgotten to be taken into the house again at night. He was 12 years old, very sagacious and affectionate, particularly handsome and never had any descendants at all equal to him in beauty. For many years he slept in our room. He was of a very amiable disposition and had as far as I am able to judge no evil propensity. He was grave but could be gay. Interpreter not only of looks and actions but often as I thought of words also. He remembered his friends at any distance of time and expressed himself with pleasure at seeing them after a long or short absence.

From the diary of THE REVEREND BENJAMIN NEWTON

WINTER

11 January 1767

GREATEST SNOW, & SEVEREST WEATHER I EVER REMEMBER.
Only one Woman at Church, Gammar Kenney, who I
asked to Dinner, with Gaffar Scot, Will Turpin, John
Seare of Eaton & Sam Pollard, the only poor Men there.
Tansley also dined in the Kitchin with them. I told the Clark to
give Notice that there would be no Service in the Afternoon, it
snowing all Day in the largest Flakes I ever saw.

From the diary of THE REVEREND WILLIAM COLE

UP ON THE HILL-SIDE THE BLEACHED PRIMROSES TREMBLED
stiffly, and there was crackling cat-ice in the cart ruts.
The freezing weather had dried every scrap of moisture off the wrinkled surface of the earth. Starving birds
followed me, for my footsteps broke the ice on the tiny frozen
woodland pools and they could get water. One deeper puddle,
where an inch of water and mud showed, was ringed with small
birds within a few minutes. The willow catkins looked very hard
and tight, and the curled crisply-thin beech leaves rustled and
scratched in the bare hedges. In a sad little grey bundle under
the leaves was a frozen squirrel; perhaps his winter hiding place
had been broken by the wood-cutters, or perhaps he was too
old and weak to live until another spring. Farther on was a
stoat, quite still as he had never been in life – his small strong
legs stretched out, as if he had gone on running and leaping
into the next world. The whole landscape was frost bleached,
colourless, and flat, even the black tarred Kentish barns had a
dull bloom over them, like the colour on a sloe in November.

DOROTHY HARTLEY, *from* Made in England

Farm chores,
December, from a
fifteenth-century
Book of Hours

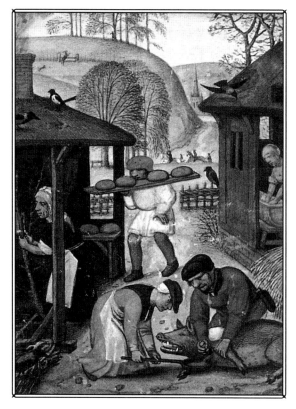

A WINTER NIGHT

With the fierce rage of winter deep suffused,
An icy gale, oft shifting, o'er the pool
Breathes a blue film, and in its mid-career
Arrests the bickering stream. The loosened ice,
Let down the flood, and half dissolved by day,
Rustles no more; but to the sedgy bank
Fast grows, or gathers round the pointed stone,
A crystal pavement, by the breath of Heaven
Cemented firm; till, seized from shore to shore,
The whole imprisoned river growls below.
Loud rings the frozen earth, and hard reflects
A double noise; while at his evening watch
The village dog deters the nightly thief;
The heifer lows; the distant water-fall

Swells in the breeze; and, with the hasty tread
Of traveller, the hollow-sounding plain
Shakes from afar. The full ethereal round,
Infinite worlds disclosing to the view,
Shines out intensely keen; and, all one cope
Of starry glitter, glows from Pole to Pole.
From Pole to Pole the rigid influence falls
Through the still night, incessant, heavy, strong,
And seizes Nature fast. It freezes on;
Till morn, late-rising o'er the drooping world,
Lifts her pale eye unjoyous.

JAMES THOMSON

GORRAN SCHOOL, WITH A HOUSE FOR 'MASTER' GLUED TO it, stood strong and symmetrical, without beauty but not mean, triumphantly facing the wrong way. It might have looked south over the distant Gruda and the sea; but this advantage was forgone in favour of presenting a good face to the road. Master's room in school, the big room as we called it, caught the north wind while the closets at the back caught the sun. I have heard that Mr Silvanus Trevail, the architect, who designed many Cornish schools, committed suicide in the end; but whether out of remorse for his cold frontages I do not know.

ANNE TRENEER, *from* School House in the Wind

13 February 1870 Septuagesima Sunday, St Valentine's Eve

PREACHED AT CLYRO IN THE MORNING (MATTHEW XIV, 30). Very few people in Church, the weather fearful, violent deadly E. wind and the hardest frost we have had yet. Went to Bettws in the afternoon wrapped in two waistcoats, two coats, a muffler and a mackintosh, and was not at all too warm. Heard the Chapel bell pealing strongly for the second time since I have been here and when I got to the Chapel my beard moustaches and whiskers were so stiff with ice that I could hardly open my mouth and my beard was frozen on to my mackintosh. There was a large christening party from Llwyn Gwilym. The baby was baptized in ice which was broken and swimming about in the Font.

From the diary of THE REVEREND FRANCIS KILVERT

IT WAS A WORLD OF GLASS, SPARKLING AND MOTIONLESS. Vapours had frozen all over the trees and transformed them into confections of sugar. Everything was rigid, locked-up and sealed, and when we breathed the air it smelt like needles and stabbed our nostrils and made us sneeze . . . The church clock had stopped and the weather-cock was frozen, so that both time and the winds were stilled; and nothing, we thought, could be more exciting than this; interference by a hand unknown, the winter's No to routine and laws – sinister, awesome, welcome.

LAURIE LEE, *from* Cider with Rosie

28 February 1785

THE FROST SEVERER THAN EVER IN THE NIGHT AS IT EVEN froze the Chamber Pots under the Beds. Wind very rough and tho' the Sun shone all the morning very bright yet it continued freezing every minute. Most bitter cold to day indeed, and likely to continue.

From the diary of THE REVEREND JAMES WOODFORDE

'WHAT'S THE MATTER, EEYORE?' . . .
'I don't know how it is, Christopher Robin, but what with all this snow and one thing and another, not to mention icicles and such-like, it isn't so Hot in my field about three o'clock in the morning as some people think it is.'

A.A. MILNE, *from* The House at Pooh Corner

THAW

Tiny immortal streams are on the move:
The sun his hand uncloses like a statue
Irrevocably. Thereby such light is freed
That all the dingy hospital of snow
Dies back to ditches. Chalkbeds of heaven bear
These nameless tributaries, but they run
To earth. For here their pouring river reigns:
Here, busy with resurrection, sovereign waters
Confer among the roots, causing to fall
From patient memory forestfuls of grief.
How easily it falls, how easily I let drift
On the surface of the morning feathers of self-reproach,
How easily I disperse the scolding of the snow.

PHILIP LARKIN

Harvesting a crop of January potatoes, 1956

GOD AND MAN

GRAVEYARD IN NORFOLK

Still in the countryside among the lowly
Death is not out of fashion,
Still is the churchyard park and promenade
And a new-made grave a glory.
Still on Sunday afternoons, contentedly and slowly,
Come widows eased of their passion,
Whose children flitting from stone to headstone façade
Spell out accustomed names and the same story.

From mound to mound chirps grasshopper to grasshopper:
John dear husband of Mary,
Ada, relict, Lydia the only child,
Seem taking part in the chatter.
With boom and stumble, with cadence and patient cropper,
The organist practises the voluntary,
Swallows rehearsing their flight sit Indian-filed,
And under the blue sky nothing is the matter.

With spruce asters and September roses
Replenished are jampots and vases,
From the breasts of the dead the dead blossoms are swept
And tossed over into the meadow.
Women wander from grave to grave inspecting the posies,
And so tranquilly time passes
One might believe the scything greybeard slept
In the yew tree's shadow.

Here for those that mourn and are heavy-laden
Is pledge of Christ's entertainment;
Here is no Monday rising from warm bed,
No washing or baking or brewing,
No fret for stubborn son or flighty maiden,
No care for food or raiment;
No sweeping or dusting or polishing need the dead,
Nothing but flowers' renewing.

Here can the widow walk and the trembling mother
And hear with the organ blended
The swallows' auguring twitter of a brief flight
To a securer staying;
Can foretaste that heavenly park where toil and pother,
Labour and sorrow ended,
They shall stroll with husband and children in blameless
    white,
In sunlight, with music playing.

SYLVIA TOWNSEND WARNER

Church Interior
by W.H. Hunt

When I am dead, and laid in grave,
And all my bones are rotten,
By this may I remembered be
When I should be forgotten.

Poem found on a girl's sampler, 1736

'WHAT BE A DUMB ANIMAL, MR FACEY?' SHE INQUIRED. 'Whatever,' replied Mr Facey, 'do bide about and say nothing.'

Lily pondered over his words . . .

Lily Topp awoke the next morning feeling hungry. She also awoke surprised, for her cot had been moved in the night, and she with it, into a small inner room.

Lily was soon in her clothes and, hearing the cottage door open and shut, she peeped from the window and saw her mother walking up the lane with a hurried step and crying as she walked.

'She bain't dumb,' said Lily, a little disappointedly.

Lily's room faced the meadow – the snared rabbit still remained there; nothing had touched it.

Lily went into the next room. Her father was in bed, but a sheet was drawn over his face.

Lily pulled the sheet back.

'Bain't 'ee going to get up, our Dad?' she called.

There was no reply and Lily became interested.

'Be thee dumb?' asked Lily. But no reply came.

'If thee be a dumb animal,' said Lily, 'who do bide about and say nothing, thee may be fed.' John Topp remained silent.

Lily went at once into the field in front of the house . . .

Farmer Denny always rose early, as a rich man should do, in order to guard his wealth from harm, and as Lily was loosing the noose from the dead rabbit's neck the heavy hand of the farmer was laid upon her shoulder.

Lily shook herself free and stood up boldly with the rabbit in her hand.

''Taint stealing,' she said, 'to take for a dumb animal.''

'And what dumb animal are you taking my rabbit for?' asked Mr Denny.

'Our Daddy do bide about and say nothing,' replied Lily.

Farmer Denny moved out of the child's way. He had heard a sound that pleaded for the dumb animal, too – the tolling of the parish bell.

T. F. POWYS, *from* A Dumb Animal

EVE

Eve, with her basket, was
Deep in the bells and grass,
Wading in bells and grass
Up to her knees,
Picking a dish of sweet
Berries and plums to eat,
Down in the bells and grass
Under the trees.

Mute as a mouse in a
Corner the cobra lay,
Curled round a bough of the
Cinnamon tall . . .
Now to get even and
Humble proud heaven and –
Now was the moment or
Never at all.

'Eva!' Each syllable
Light as a flower fell,
'Eva!' he whispered the
Wondering maid,
Soft as a bubble sung
Out of a linnet's lung,

Soft and most silverly
'Eva!' he said.

Picture that orchard sprite,
Eve, with her body white,
Supple and smooth to her
Slim finger tips,
Wondering, listening,
Listening, wondering,
Eve with a berry
Half-way to her lips.

Oh, had our simple Eve
Seen through the make-believe!
Had she but known the
Pretender he was!
Out of the boughs he came,
Whispering still her name,
Tumbling in twenty rings
Into the grass.

Here was the strangest pair
In the world anywhere,
Eve in the bells and grass
Kneeling, and he
Telling his story low . . .
Singing birds saw them go
Down the dark path to
The Blasphemous Tree.

Oh, what a clatter when
Titmouse and Jenny Wren
Saw him successful and
Taking his leave!
How the birds rated him,
How they all hated him!
How they all pitied
Poor motherless Eve!

175

Picture her crying,
Outside in the lane,
Eve, with no dish of sweet
Berries and plums to eat,
Haunting the gate of the
Orchard in vain . . .
Picture the lewd delight
Under the hill to-night –
'Eva!' the toast goes round,
'Eva!' again.

RALPH HODGSON

I WAS VERY MUCH VEXED WITH THE APE, AND TOLD IT SO IN NO uncertain manner. The gardener said he would know what to do to it if it was his, and looked at his stick, but I did not approve of corporal punishment and would not thrash it. Instead, I spoke to it very sharply, and chained it up for the rest of the day and gave it the dullest kind of food, and did not take it out driving for two days, and then did all the driving myself, which always vexed it. It seemed ashamed of itself, and I thought it was increasing in conscience and sense of sin. I was teaching it a little religion (Anglican), which Meg thought was wrong, her Church being rather narrow about animals, and she would not have allowed it to go with her to her church, but I took it, on the lead, to mine, where it behaved quite well, sitting and standing and kneeling when I did, and it was a great interest to the congregation and choir at Mass, but the vicar did not care for it, he thought it distracted people's attention and was not really reverent. It always rather enjoyed being an object of interest, as it was vain and exhibitionist, but how much it knew about where it was, I did not know. I liked the way it fell on its knees at the right place in the creed, seeing other people do it and not waiting to be pulled. When the congregation made the responses and joined in the service, it joined too, softly chattering. I taught it to genuflect as I did when we went in to our seats. Soon I saw that it was crossing itself too, and I was not quite sure that it ought to be doing this, it seemed going rather far, but it liked it, and did it again and again, even when no one else did, its tendency to excess and showing off coming out as usual, and the vicar and the churchwardens did not much like this. It was certainly a very devout Anglo-Catholic, though I fancied that it might be also something of an Anglo-Agnostic. During the sermon it leant against me and fell asleep, snoring a little, because it was rather old-fashioned, and possibly something of an anti-clerical too. I thought it was a very fine convert from the Moslem religion, to which I suppose it had nominally belonged before. But I suspected that if any one took it to a Billy Graham meeting, it would follow the crowd up and decide for conversion in a rather impulsive and shallow way, and I remembered the parrot in the seventeenth century play which was converted to Calvinism by a serving-woman.

> *Yesterday I went*
> *To see a lady that has a parrot; my woman converted*
> *the fowl,*
> *And now it can speak naught but Knox's words;*
> *So there's a parrot lost.*
> ROSE MACAULAY, *from* The Towers of Trebizond

DEATH

Flowers shall hang upon the palls,
Brighter than patterns upon shawls,
And blossoms shall be in the coffin lids,
Sadder than tears on grief's eyelids,
Garlands shall hide pale corpses' faces
When beauty shall rot in charnel places,
Spring flowers shall come in dews of sorrow
For the maiden goes down to her grave to-morrow.

Last week she went walking and stepping along,
Gay as first flowers of spring or the tune of a song;
Her eye was as bright as the sun in its calm,
Her lips they were rubies, her bosom was warm,
And white as the snowdrop that lies on her breast;
Now death like a dream is her bedfellow guest,
And white as the sheets—ay and paler than they,
Now her face in its beauty has perished to clay.

Spring flowers they shall hang on her pall,
More bright than the pattern that bloomed on her shawl,
And blooms shall be strown where the corpse lies hid,
More sad than the tears upon grief's eyelid;
And ere the return of another sweet May
She'll be rotting to dust in the coffined clay,
And the grave whereon the bright snowdrops grow
Shall be the same soil as the beauty below.

JOHN CLARE

A TOMBSTONE EPITAPH

Between the Remains of her Brother EDWARD
And of her Husband ARTHUR
Here lies the Body of BRIDGETT APPLEWHAITE
Once BRIDGETT NELSON.
After the Fatigues of a Married Life,
Born by her with Incredible Patience,
For four years and three Quarters, bating three Weeks,
And after the Enjoiment of the Glorious Freedom
Of an Early and Unblemisht Widowhood,
For four Years and Upwards,
She Resolved to run the Risk of a Second Marriage-Bed
But DEATH forbad the Banns —
And having with an Apoplectick Dart
(The same Instrument, with which he had Formerly

Dispatch't her Mother),
Touch't the most Vital part of her Brain;
She must have fallen Directly to the Ground,
(as one Thunder-strook)
If she had not been Catch't and Supported
by her Intended Husband.
Of which Invisible Bruise,
After a Struggle, for above Sixty Hours
With that Grand Enemy to Life,
(But the Certain and Mercifull Friend to Helpless Old
Age,)
In Terrible Convulsions, Plaintive Groans, or Stupefying
Sleep,
Without recovery of her Speech, or Senses,
She Dyed, on the 12th Day of Sept: in ye Year
of our Lord, 1737
and
of her own age, 44.

Behold! I come as a Thief, Rev. 16th Chr., 15th v.

THE COUNTRY CLERGY

I see them working in old rectories
By the sun's light, by candlelight,
Venerable men, their black cloth
A little dusty, a little green
With holy mildew. And yet their skulls,
Ripening over so many prayers,
Toppled into the same grave
With oafs and yokels. They left no books,
Memorial to their lonely thought
In grey parishes; rather they wrote
On men's hearts and in the minds
Of young children sublime words

Too soon forgotten. God in his time
Or out of time will correct this.

R. S. THOMAS

My dear Penelope,

I HAVE BEEN THINKING OVER THE QUESTION OF THE PLAYING of the harmonium on Sunday evenings here and have reached the conclusion that I must now take it over myself.

I am very grateful to you for doing it for so long and hate to have to ask you to give it up, but, to put it plainly, your playing has got worse and worse and the disaccord between the harmonium and the congregation is becoming destructive of devotion. People are not very sensitive here, but even some of them have begun to complain, and they are not usually given to doing that. I do not like writing this, but I think you will understand that it is my business to see that divine worship is as perfect as it can be made. Perhaps the crankiness of the instrument has something to do with the trouble. I think it does require a careful and experienced player to deal with it.

Thank you ever so much for stepping so generously into the breach when Sibyl was ill; it was the greatest possible help to me and your results were noticeably better then than now.

Yours ever,
F. P. Harton

F.P. HARTON, *letter to Penelope Betjeman*

THE VILLAGE

Up yonder hill, behold how sadly slow
The bier moves winding from the vale below;
There lie the happy dead, from trouble free,
And the glad parish pays the frugal fee:

No more, O Death! thy victim starts to hear
Churchwarden stern, or kingly overseer;
No more the farmer claims his humble bow,
Thou art his lord, the best of tyrants thou!
    Now to the church behold the mourners come,
Sedately torpid and devoutly dumb;
The village children now their games suspend,
To see the bier that bears their ancient friend;
For he was one in all their idle sport,
And like a monarch ruled their little court.
The pliant bow he form'd, the flying ball,
The bat, the wicket, were his labours all;
Him now they follow to his grave, and stand,
Silent and sad, and gazing, hand in hand;
While bending low, their eager eyes explore
The mingled relics of the parish poor.
The bell tolls late, the moping owl flies round,
Fear marks the flight and magnifies the sound;
The busy priest, detain'd by weightier care,
Defers his duty till the day of prayer;
And, waiting long, the crowd retire distress'd,
To think a poor man's bones should lie unbless'd.

GEORGE CRABBE

May 1874

THEN THE VICAR OF FORDINGTON TOLD US OF THE STATE
of things in his parish when he first came to it nearly
half a century ago. No man had ever been known to
receive the Holy Communion except the parson, the sexton
and the clerk. There were 16 women communicants and most
of them went away when he refused to pay them for coming.

They had been accustomed there at some place in the
neighbourhood to pass the cup to each other with a nod of the
head. At one church there were two male communicants. When

the cup was given to the first, he touched his forelock and said, 'Here's your good health, Sir.' The other said, 'Here's the good health of our Lord Jesus Christ.'

Oner day there was a christening, and no water in the font. 'Water, Sir!' said the clerk in astonishment. 'The last parson never used no water! He spit into his hand!'

The Bishop of Oxford, 1902

From the diary of THE REVEREND FRANCIS KILVERT

EASTER

I got me flowers to straw thy way,
I got me boughs off many a tree:
But thou wast up by break of day,
And brought'st thy sweets along with thee.

The Sun arising in the East,
Though he give light, and the East perfume,
If they should offer to contest
With thy arising, they presume.

Can there be any day but this,
Though many sunnes to shine endeavour?
We count three hundred, but we misse:
There is but one, and that one ever.

GEORGE HERBERT

SOCIETY

H E FOUND THE NEIGHBOURHOOD MUCH THE SAME AS ALL other neighbourhoods: 'Red wine and white, soup and fish, bad wit and good nature.'

HESKETH PEARSON, *from* The Smith of Smiths

N OTICE, FOR INSTANCE, THE WOMEN WHO HAVE DONE their shopping in the town early in the morning, and are coming home for a day's work. They are out of breath, and bothered with their armfuls of purchases; but nine times out of ten their faces look hopeful; there is no sound of grievance or of worry in their talk; their smiling 'Good-morning' to you proves somehow that it is not a bad morning with them. One day a woman going to the town a little late met another already returning, loaded up with goods. ''Ullo, Mrs Fry,' she laughed, 'you be 'bliged to be fust, then?' 'Yes; but I en't bought it *all*; I thought you'd be comin', so I left some for you.' 'That's right of ye. En't it a *nice mornin'*?' 'Jest what we wants! My old man was up an' in he's garden . . . ' The words grow indistinguishable as you get farther away; you don't hear what the 'old man' was doing so early, but the country voices sound for a long time, comfortably tuned to the pleasantness of the day.

This sort of thing is so common that I seldom notice it, unless it is varied in some way that attracts attention. For instance, I could not help listening to a woman who was pushing her baby in a perambulator down the hill. The baby sat facing her, as bland as a little image of Buddha, and as unresponsive, but she was chaffing it. 'Well, you *be* a funny little gal, *ben't* ye? Why, you be goin' back'ards into the town! Whoever heared tell o' such a thing – goin' to the town *back*'ards. You *be* a funny little gal!' To me it was a funny little procession, with a touch of the pathetic hidden away in it somewhere; but it bore convincing witness to happiness in at least one home in our valley.

GEORGE BOURNE, *from* Change in the Village

24 March Coleridge, the Chesters, and Ellen Cruikshank called. We walked with them through the wood. Went in the evening into the Coombe to get eggs; returned through the wood, and walked in the park. A duller night than last night: a sort of white shade over the blue sky. The stars dim. The spring continues to advance very slowly, no green trees, the hedges leafless, nothing green but the brambles that still retain their old leaves, the evergreens, and the palms, which indeed are not absolutely green. Some brambles I observed to-day budding afresh, and those have shed their old leaves. The crooked arm of the old oak tree points upwards to the moon.

25 March Walked to Coleridge's after tea. Arrived at home at one o'clock. The night cloudy but not dark.

26 March Went to meet Wedgwood at Coleridge's after dinner. Reached home at half-past twelve, a fine moonlight night; half moon.

27 March Dined at Poole's. Arrived at home a little after twelve, a partially cloudy, but light night, very cold.

28 March Hung out the linen.

29 March Coleridge dined with us.

30 March Walked I know not where.

31 March Walked.

1 April Walked by moonlight.

DOROTHY WORDSWORTH, Journals

JUST THEN MR HOLBROOK APPEARED AT THE DOOR, RUBBING his hands in very effervescence of hospitality. He looked more like my idea of Don Quixote than ever, and yet the likeness was only external. His respectable housekeeper stood modestly at the door to bid us welcome; and while she led the elder ladies upstairs to a bedroom, I begged to look about the garden. My request evidently pleased the old gentleman; who took me all round the place, and showed me his six-and-twenty cows, named after the different letters of the alphabet . . .

When he and I went in, we found that dinner was nearly ready in the kitchen,—for so I suppose the room ought to be called, as there were oak dressers and cupboards all round, an oven by the side of the fireplace, and only a small Turkey carpet in the middle of the flag-floor . . .

When the ducks and green peas came, we looked at each other in dismay; we had only two-pronged, black-handled forks. It is true, the steel was as bright as silver; but what were we to do? Miss Matty picked up her peas, one by one, on the point of the prongs, much as Aminé ate her grains of rice after her previous feast with the Ghoul. Miss Pole sighed over her delicate young peas as she left them on one side of her plate untasted; for they *would* drop between the prongs. I looked at my host: the peas were going wholesale into his capacious mouth, shovelled up by his large round-ended knife. I saw, I imitated, I survived! My friends, in spite of my precedent, could not muster up courage enough to do an ungenteel thing; and, if Mr Holbrook had not been so heartily hungry, he would probably have seen that the good peas went away almost untouched.

After dinner, a clay pipe was brought in, and a spittoon; and, asking us to retire to another room, where he would soon join us, if we disliked tobacco-smoke, he presented his pipe to Miss Matty, and requested her to fill the bowl. This was a compliment to a lady in his youth; but it was rather inappropriate to propose it as an honour to Miss Matty, who had been trained by her sister to hold smoking of every kind in utter abhorrence. But if it was a shock to her refinement, it was also a gratification

Farmer Giles and
his wife shewing
off their
daughter Betty *by
James Gillray,
1809*

to her feelings to be thus selected; so she daintily stuffed the
strong tobacco into the pipe; and then we withdrew.

'It is very pleasant dining with a bachelor,' said Miss Matty,
softly, as we settled ourselves in the counting-house. 'I only
hope it is not improper; so many pleasant things are!'

ELIZABETH GASKELL, *from* Cranford

AT OUR VILLAGE INN THIS WINTER THERE HAVE BEEN
balls which have been attended by many of the servants
of neighbouring families, in which, I understand, the
females have displayed a style of dress out of character to their
situation in life. Whilst the wife of the Butler of a gentleman's
family in our parish applied to me for a charitable donation of
childbed linnen, the laundry or kitchen maid in the same
family, I heard, was at this ball in the following attire. A striped
blue gauze dress trimmed with blue and white sattin wreathes,

blond nett long sleeves, blue bracelets, long blue sash, blue roses in her head, a gold chain and coral necklace, silk stockings and white gloves and shoes. Other dresses, it seems, were in the same style.

From the diary of PENELOPE HIND

O H! MY DEAR SIR, DON'T YOU FIND THAT NINE PARTS OF the world in ten are no use but to make you wish yourself with that tenth part? I am so far from growing used to mankind by living among them, that my natural ferocity does but every day grow worse.

They tire me, they fatigue me; I don't know what to do with them; I don't know what to say to them; I fling open the windows, and fancy I want air; and when I get by myself, I undress myself and seem to have had people in my pockets, in my plaits, and on my shoulders! Indeed I find this fatigue worse in the country than in the town, because one can avoid it there and has more resources; but it is there too.

I fear 'tis growing old: but I literally seem to have murdered a man whose name was Ennui, for his ghost is ever before me. They say there is no English word for 'ennui': I think you may translate it most literally by what is called 'entertaining people' and 'doing the honours': that is, you sit an hour with somebody you don't know and don't care for, talk about the wind and the weather, and ask a thousand foolish questions, which all begin with 'I think you live a good deal in the country' or 'I think you don't love this thing or that'. Oh! 'tis dreadful!

HORACE WALPOLE, *fourth Earl of Orford*

September 20th. — Letter from County Secretary of adjoining County, telling me that she knows how busy I am – which I'm certain she doesn't – but Women's Institutes of Chick, Little

March, and Crimpington find themselves in terrible difficulty owing to uncertainty about next month's speaker. Involved fragments about son coming, or not coming, home on leave from Patagonia, and daughter ill – but not dangerously – at Bromley, Kent – follow. President is away – (further fragment, about President being obliged to visit aged relative while aged relative's maid is on holiday) – and County Secretary does not know what to do. What she does do, however, is to suggest that I should be prepared to come and speak at all three Institute meetings, if – as she rather strangely puts it – the worst comes to the worst. Separate half-sheet of paper gives details about dates, times, and bus between Chick and Little March, leading on to doctor's sister's two-seater, at cross-roads between Little March and Crimpington Hill. At Crimpington, County Secretary concludes triumphantly, I shall be put up for the night by Lady Magdalen Crimp – always so kind, and such a friend to the Movement – at Crimpington Hall. *P.S.* Travel talks always popular, but anything I like will be delightful. Chick very keen about Folk Lore, Little March more on the Handicraft side. *But anything I like. P.P.S.* Would I be so kind as to judge Recitation Competition at Crimpington?

E. M. DELAFIELD, from Diary of a Provincial Lady

1 August 1719

I RODE HOME TO SEE MY HAY-MAKING; AND WILL CLARKE AND another Man who were making a Rick in Westley's Wood were both very fast asleep upon the top of a Load of Hay standing by the Rick in my Wagon.

Later I was at our Musick-Meeting; and Mr Ducket of Caune in Wiltshire play'd on a Flute one song with us: But Mr Hill's Harpsichord being near a note below Consort Pitch, and no sure Hand performing the Trebles (being only young Ladds of Wells and Shepton,) our Musick was very mean.

From the diary of DR CLAVER MORRIS

VISITING WAS A FAVOURITE GAME WITH SUSAN AND ME ON wet winter Saturday afternoons. We called this game 'young ladies'. Susan would have our bedroom, I would have the boys' bedroom – the boys being safely out rabbiting with my father at Beeparks. We would divide the dolls and get out our tea-sets. Then we dressed up in mother's clothes or in long dresses made of old curtains. We turned out discarded veils and jet bracelets, and carried old sunshades with deep fringes. We then took turns to visit each other, knocking at each other's doors, being admitted, being taken to the equivalent of the spare bedroom to remove our veils, and sitting down sometimes to an imaginary tea, sometimes, if mother were in a good mood, to real little bits of cake, and a mock blanc-mange made of moist sugar, pressed into an egg-cup and turned out as though from a 'shape'. I forget all the proceedings, but I do remember we always finished by dancing Sir Roger de Coverley together, holding up our long dresses and doing all the figures, and taking all the parts of all the couples. One or other of us in these games would be Mrs Williams at the castle. How we longed for a curled fringe!

ANNE TRENEER, *from* School House in the Wind

THE WHOLE PARTY WERE ASSEMBLED, EXCEPTING FRANK Churchill, who was expected every moment from Richmond; and Mrs Elton, in all her apparatus of happiness, her large bonnet and her basket, was very ready to lead the way in gathering, accepting, or talking—strawberries, and only strawberries, could now be thought or spoken of. 'The best fruit in England—every body's favourite—always whole-some. These the finest beds and finest sorts. Delightful to gather for one's self—the only way of really enjoying them. Morning decidedly the best time—never tired—every sort good—hautboy infinitely superior—no comparison—the others hardly eatable—hautboys very scarce—Chili preferred—white wood finest flavour of all—price of strawberries

OVERLEAF: *A family picnic at Sulham House, c. 1889*

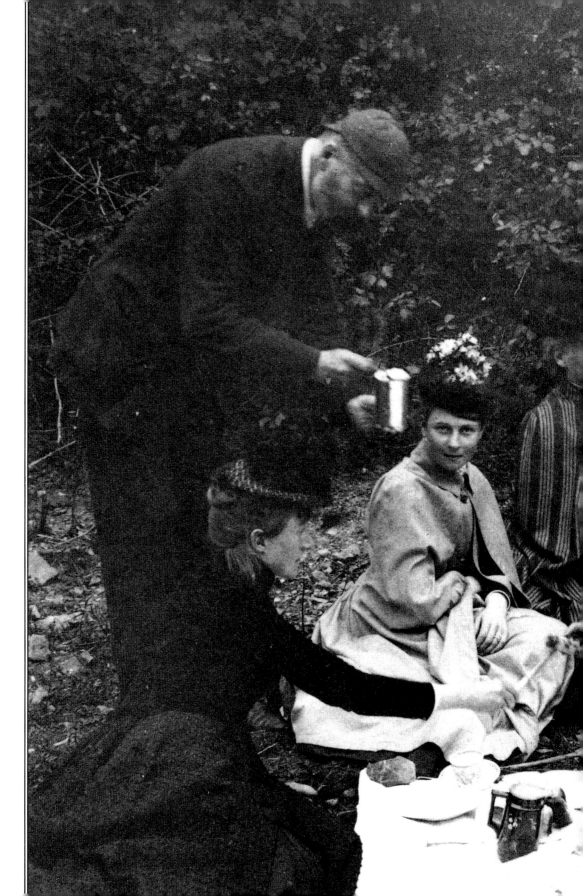

in London—abundance about Bristol—Maple Grove—cultivation—beds when to be renewed—gardeners thinking exactly different—no general rule—gardeners never to be put out of their way—delicious fruit—only too rich to be eaten much of—inferior to cherries—currants more refreshing—only objection to gathering strawberries the stooping—glaring sun—tired to death—could bear it no longer—must go and sit in the shade.'

JANE AUSTEN, *from* Emma

23 May, 1835

O N MONDAY I WENT TO PETWORTH AND SAW THE FINEST fête that could be given. Lord Egremont had been accustomed some time in the winter to feast the poor of the adjoining parishes (women and children, not men) in the riding house and tennis court, where they were admitted by relays.

His illness prevented the dinner taking place, but when he recovered he was bent upon having it, and, as it was put off till the summer, he had arranged it in the open air, and a fine sight it was: fifty-four tables, each fifty feet long, were placed in a vast semi-circle on the lawn before the house. Nothing could be more amusing than to look at the preparations. The tables were all spread with cloths, and plates, and dishes; two great tents were erected in the middle to receive the provisions, which were conveyed in carts, like ammunition. Plum puddings and loaves were piled like cannon balls, and innumerable joints of boiled and roast beef were spread out, while hot joints were prepared in the kitchen, and sent forth as soon as the firing of the guns announced the hour of the feast. Tickets were given to the inhabitants of a certain district, and the number was about 4,000; but, as many more came, the old Peer could not endure that there should be anybody hungering outside his gates, and he went out himself and ordered the barriers to be taken down and admittance given to all. They think 6,000 were fed. Gentlemen from the neighbourhood carved for them, and waiters were provided from among the peasantry. The food was distributed from the tents and carried off upon hurdles to all parts of the semi-circle. A band of music paraded round playing gay airs. The day was glorious – an unclouded sky and soft southern breeze. Nothing could exceed the pleasure of that fine old fellow: he was in and out of the window of his room twenty times, enjoying the sight of these poor wretches, all attired in their best, cramming themselves and their brats with as much as they could devour, and snatching a day of relaxation and happiness.

From the diary of CHARLES GREVILLE

WE HAVE HAD A SPIRT OF COMPANY FOR THE LAST THREE days, but they all very kindly walked off yesterday, and as it is wrong to dwell upon past evils, I spare you an account of most of them.

There were a Mr and Mrs Wynyard among them who were very pleasant. He was in the Army, but is now in the Church, and though they are the sort of people who have a child every year, and talk about their governess, and though she very naturally imagined, that because she was absent, the high wind would blow away the little tituppy parsonage, and the precious children, yet they really were very agreeable.

EMILY EDEN, *letter to the Dowager Lady Buckinghamshire, 1819*

10 February 1873

THE DALLINS CALLED. THEY LEAVE FOR DEVONSHIRE ON Wednesday. Mrs Dallin forces her hyacinths on the kitchen hob, to the great disgust of the cook, and Mrs

Dallin expects that some day the cook in revenge will send up the hyacinths for dinner dressed as vegetables. Mrs Dallin is also raising snowdrops from *seed*.

My Mother says that at Dursley in Gloucestershire, when ladies and gentlemen used to go out to dinner together on dark nights, the gentlemen pulled out the tails of their shirts and walked before to show the way and light the ladies. These were called 'Dursley lanterns'.

From the diary of THE REVEREND FRANCIS KILVERT

I SHALL BE EXTREMELY HAPPY TO SEE HARRY, AND WILL LEAVE a note for him at the tavern where the Mail stops to say so. Nothing can exceed the dullness of this place and this family: but he has been accustomed to living alone with his grandmother, which, though a highly moral life, is not a very amusing one. There are Scotch ladies staying here with whom he will get acquainted, and to whom he may safely make love the ensuing winter; for love, though a very acute disorder in Andalucia, puts on a very chronic shape in these high northern latitudes: for first the lover must prove *metapheezically* that he ought to; and then, in the fifth or sixth year of courtship, or rather argument, if the summer is tolerably warm and oatmeal plenty, the fair one yields.

THE REVEREND SYDNEY SMITH,
letter to Lady Holland, 1829

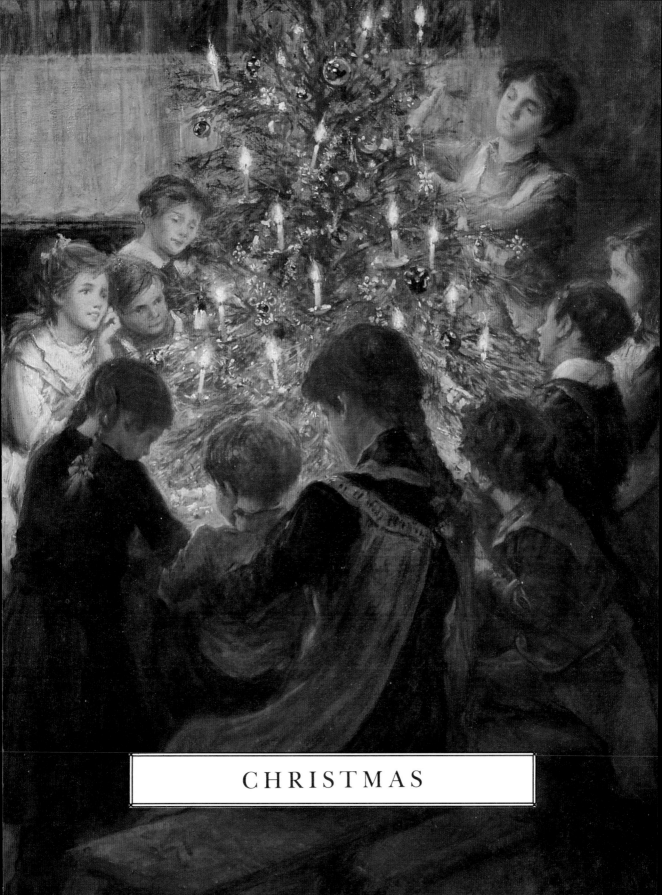

CHRISTMAS

PREVIOUS PAGE: The Christmas Tree *by A. Chevallier Taylor*

A CAROL

Our Lord Who did the Ox command
   To kneel to Judah's King,
He binds His frost upon the land
   To ripen it for Spring–
To ripen it for Spring, good sirs,
   According to His word;
Which well must be as ye can see–
   And who shall judge the Lord?

When we poor fenmen skate the ice
   Or shiver on the wold,
We hear the cry of a single tree
   That breaks her heart in the cold–
That breaks her heart in the cold, good sirs
   And rendeth by the board;
Which well must be as ye can see–
   And who shall judge the Lord?

Her wood is crazed and little worth
   Excepting as to burn,
That we may warm and make our mirth
   Until the Spring return–
Until the Spring return, good sirs,
   When people walk abroad;
Which well must be as ye can see–
   And who shall judge the Lord?

God bless the master of this house,
   And all that sleep therein!
And guard the fens from pirate folk,
   And keep us all from sin,
To walk in honesty, good sirs,
   Of thought and deed and word!
Which shall befriend our latter end–
   And who shall judge the Lord?

RUDYARD KIPLING

ALL THE CHRISTMASES ROLL DOWN THE HILL TOWARDS THE Welsh-speaking sea, like a snowball growing whiter and bigger and rounder, like a cold and headlong moon bundling down the sky that was our street; and they stop at the rim of the ice-edged, fish-freezing waves, and I plunge my hands in the snow and bring out whatever I can find; holly or robins or pudding, squabbles and carols and oranges and tin whistles.

DYLAN THOMAS, *from* Memories of Christmas

THE BEST PART OF CHRISTMAS DAY WAS THE WALK TO Gruda with my father after the late midday dinner, and the coming in after it to tea in the parlour. Tea was in the parlour on Christmas Days. Commonly when my mother had tea in the parlour with a friend the children had it together in the kitchen – there were three doors, a passage and a room between. There is a story that once when mother was wielding her best silver teapot and enjoying Mrs Kendal's company the door was suddenly burst open and a very dirty Cap'n appeared

Children carol singing, from Book of Days *by R. Chambers*

saying, 'Mother, Howard's got tart; why can't I have tart? I want tart.' But on Christmas Day we were all exalted to the best room for tea, and it was a tea after our heart's desire. We did not stay up to supper on Christmas night. Our parents must have been glad to get rid of us. After tea we played games and sang, and ate almonds and muscatels and roasted chestnuts. Then we went into the dark dining-room and, for the second time, lit the candles on our tree. But the glory had departed; it was never quite the same the second night. We let the candles burn right down, and the splendour of Christmas was over. Though the decorations remained up, and the tree was left standing till Twelfth Night, all had grown ordinary.

ANNE TRENEER, from School House in the Wind

25 December 1866

MARRIED A YOUNG PARISHIONER OF THE NAME OF Mahershallalashbaz Tuck. He accounted for the possession of so extraordinary a name thus: his father wished to call him by the shortest name in the Bible, and for that purpose selected Uz. But, the clergyman making some demur, the father said in pique, 'Well, if he cannot have the shortest he shall have the longest.'

From the diary of THE REVEREND BENJAMIN ARMSTRONG

CHRISTMAS FAMILY REUNION

Since last the tutelary hearth
Has seen the bursting pod of kin,
I've thought how good the family mould,
How solid and how genuine.

Now once again the aunts are here,
The uncles, sisters, brothers,
With candy in the children's hair
And grown-ups in each other's.

There's talk of saving room for pie,
Grandma discusses her neuralgia;
I long for time to pass, so I
Can think of all this with nostalgia.

PETER DE VRIES

TO MAKE PIES

PARBOILE YOUR MUTTON, THEN TAKE AS MUCH SUET AS meat, & mince it both small, then put mace & nutmegs & cinnamon, & sugar & orinnges peels, & currance & great reasins, & a little rose water, put all these to the meat, beat yor spice & orinnge peels very small, & mingle yor fruit & spice & all togither, with the meat, & so bake it, put as much currance as meat & twice so much sugar as salt, put some ginger into it, let the suet bee beef suet, for it is better than mutton suet.

LADY ELINOR FETTIPLACE, 1604

WELL, IT'S OVER, THE ANNUAL GUZZLE, PEELING ALL those bright wrappings from presents, stringing up gay cards destined all too soon for the dustbin. So much care, skill and effort has gone into the production of those cards, and some are so attractive (Old Masters and birds and beasts particularly) that it goes to my heart to throw them away. Often I've kept a few favourite ones, to be used perhaps as book-markers, but in the end they clutter desk or drawer and must go. What a world of waste we inhabit.

The cottage reverberates with stentorian commands. 'NO, Jos, that frog is Alexander's,' 'Leave Hugh's rabbit ALONE.' Jos has taken to letting off steam almost literally, with a piercing high-pitched yell like a demonic engine. When the boiler and the cats join in and the radio's going, even the Red Arrows couldn't make themselves heard.

The painted wooden angels have come out of the loft for their annual outing. They see the light for about three days and then hibernate, and aestivate, for the rest of the year, like characters in some Greek myth about fertility. They must be forty years old, bought for a few dollars on Madison Avenue and gradually matured into a family tradition. All with trumpets, wings and halos. One has lost her halo over the years.

Rain all day, thinning to a drizzle and then surging back into a storm. An afternoon walk across sodden fields towards the Swill Brook, all deserted, no cattle in the fields, only rooks flying over, an occasional blackbird chattering in a bare hedge, a solitary heron flapping slowly. It might have been the heron who deposited in the middle of a field a grey bivalve, former home of a Swan mussel.

ELSPETH HUXLEY, *from* Gallipot Eyes

THERE WERE TWO CHRISTMAS TREES, ONE AT EACH END OF the long drawing-room, and on these trees there was a present – an expensive one, too! – for every one of us. And there was a hired band and we danced the polka and the lancers and gallops – which were the greatest possible fun – and waltzes, which everyone, except the rather elderly who asked each other solemnly 'Do you reverse?', found rather boring, for the young grown-up people wanted to dance the two-step and we children demanded Sir Roger de Coverley.

But Sir Roger was, by tradition, kept back for the last dance of all – a dance in which everyone, old, middle-aged and young, joined, clapping our hands and jostling each other till the sweat poured out of us and we all agreed it was 'jolly decent', which was the highest praise we knew in those days.

In the course of the evening there were carols on gramophone records and, all the time, there was food of the most exotic kinds which, topped up by innumerable glasses of 'cup', made our little stomachs distend shockingly and gave us the hiccups and were the prelude for some of the feebler ones for hurried trips to the lavatory where they were promptly sick; but, like the Romans we were in those days, we did not, after our vomiting, scuttle away, shamefaced, home, but came up for more. More dancing, more cup, more ices and fruit salad and trifle that was, surely, three parts sherry.

But, at last, just before midnight (for this was essentially a children's party), we all joined hands and those of us who knew the words sang 'Auld Lang Syne' and those of us who didn't made odd noises that we hoped would pass muster. And then it was coats and mufflers and saying goodbye and thank you to our adult hosts, while Olive and Norman, their flaming red heads like little beacons, stood at the doorway and gravely shook hands with us and thanked us for coming and hoped we had enjoyed ourselves.

So, out into the frosty night we all trooped, some to go home in motor-cars and some to pile into Race and Scott's station waggon that was to make a round of Frinton, depositing here and there these belated revellers, and some, who lived not too distantly, to walk.

At the gate into the drive we turned back to wave to Olive and Norman, still standing framed in the doorway, with the lights from the house behind them and with a surround of Japanese lanterns that, even after all these hours of revelry, still flickered away cheerfully.

It had, we agreed, been a jolly decent party. And Olive's and Norman's parents were, we agreed, jolly decent people. And Olive and Norman had been jolly decent too.

Thus, replete and sleepy and rather bilious, we recapitulated the delights of that evening.

SIMON DEWES, *from* Essex Schooldays

WASSAIL SONG

We have been a walking
   Among the leaves so green,
And hither we are coming
   So stately to be seen.

   With our wassel,
   Our jolly wassel,
   All joys come to you
   And to our wassel bowl.

Good Master and good Mistress,
   As you sit by the fire,
Remember us poor wassellers
   That travel in the mire.

Our bowl is made
   Of the mulberry tree,
So so is your ale
   Of the best barley.

Pray rise up, master Butler,
   And put on your golden ring,
And bring to us a jug of ale,
   The better we shall sing.

Our purse it is made
   Of the finest calves skin,
We want a little silver
   To line it well within.

Good Master, good Mistress,
   If that you are but willing,
Send down two of your little boys
   To each of us a shilling.

OVERLEAF:
Wassailing the
apple trees,
Somerset, on
Twelfth Night,
1931

We'll hang a silver napkin
Upon a golden spear,
And come no more a wasselling
Until another year.

ANON

So now we wait for the year to end. I like to be outside at this time. It seems a better place from which to feel the weakening pulse, to hold onto something before it is gone. Often there is no particular weather in these days between, no movement in the trees, no dogs barking. How quiet the garden seems without the geese.

There is no need for wild festivity on New Year's Eve: the time is quite potent enough. As midnight approaches, the back door of the scullery is opened into black silence for the old year to go out. Then the front door is flung open for the new one to come in. You can feel it rushing through the house like a wind. From churches at Forden, Montgomery and Berriew the ringing of bells comes crashing through the air, call changes and Bob Doubles slicing the night into arcs. And we stand self-consciously, as if something has happened, laughing not with relief or reluctance, just at the resumption of the natural order, the starting of the clock again.

'And when does the future become the present?' we used to ask. And they answered, 'Now.'

HELEN GUNN, in Country Life, 26 December 1991

BIOGRAPHICAL NOTES

Addison, Joseph (1672–1719), a distinguished classical scholar and writer. Co-founder of the *Spectator*, he was also a Whig MP from 1706 to his death.

Armstrong, Revd Benjamin (1817–90), vicar of East Dereham, Norfolk.

Ashmole, Elias (1617–92), antiquarian and astrologer, he held several government posts. In 1682 he gave his collection of curiosities to Oxford University, and thereby founded the Ashmolean Museum.

Austen, Jane (1775–1817), novelist.

Baker, J.A., writer and naturalist.

Betjeman, John (1906–84), poet, appointed poet laureate in 1972.

Binyon, Laurence (1869–1945), poet and dramatist; assistant keeper in the department of prints and drawings at the British Museum in 1909.

Blake, William (1757–1827), poet, engraver and painter.

Bourne, George (1863–1927), writer, born George Sturt, the son of a wheelwright in Farnham, Surrey, he ran the family business as well as writing many books about life in the English countryside. He took his pen name, Bourne, from the village he wrote about in *Change in the Village*.

Bradley, Richard (*c.* 1688–1732), Professor of Botany at Cambridge and Fellow of the Royal Society, he was also the author of *The Country Housewife and Lady's Directory*, published in 1727.

Bridges, Robert (1844–1930), appointed poet laureate in 1913, he was one of the founders of the Society for Pure English.

Brontë, Charlotte (1816–55), novelist.

Brontë, Emily (1818–48), novelist.

Brown, Nicholas (1722–97), Coroner for the county of Northumberland.

Butler, Lady Eleanor (1739–1829), one of the 'Ladies of Llangollen', the other being Sarah Ponsonby with whom she eloped to Plas Newydd in North Wales, where they lived contentedly until the end of their lives.

Clare, John (1793–1864), poet, the son of a labourer, he too worked as a hedge-setter and day labourer. In 1832 he left his native cottage for another, only four miles away, but the move proved deeply disturbing and in 1837 he was admitted to an asylum. He was to remain in mental institutions until his death.

Cobbett, Anne (19th C), author of *The English Housekeeper*, published in 1851.

Cobbett, William (1763–1835), radical journalist and essayist, he was the son of a farmer and entirely self-educated. In 1832 he became MP for Oldham.

Cole, William (1714–82), parish priest of Blechley, Buckinghamshire.

Coleridge, Hartley (1796–1849), poet and contributor to literary journals, he was the eldest son of Samuel Taylor Coleridge.

Coleridge, Samuel Taylor (1772–1834), poet and critic.

Cowper, William (1731–1800), poet. Called to the bar in 1754, he subsequently suffered a severe breakdown and was to be plagued by bouts of depression for the rest of his life, finding solace in evangelical Christianity.

Crabbe, George (1754–1832), poet, writer and clergyman. Before his ordination and his career as a writer he practised as a doctor in Aldeburgh.

Delafield, E.M. (1890–1943), pen-name of Edmée Elizabeth Monica Dashwood, journalist, novelist and magistrate.

de la Mare, Walter (1873–1956), poet, novelist and anthologist.

Dewes, Simon (b.1909), the son and grandson of country doctors in Hadleigh, his family has lived in East Anglia for more than seven centuries.

de Vries, Peter (b.1910), poet and writer.

Dyott, General William (1761–1846), as a soldier he served in Ireland, Nova Scotia and the West Indies; he became aide-de-camp to George III.

Eden, Emily (1797–1869), daughter of William Eden, first Baron Auckland, she accompanied her brother to India in 1835 when he was appointed governor-general. Her letters and novels reflect the social and political set of the day.

Fettiplace, Lady Elinor (*c.* 1574–1647), the wife of Sir Richard Fettiplace of Appleton Manor in Oxfordshire, her *Receipt Book* was handed down from generation to generation of her family.

Gaskell, Elizabeth (1810–65), novelist, she was also the first biographer of her friend, Charlotte Brontë.

Gissing, George (1857–1903), writer and novelist, most notably the author of *New Grub Street*.

Grahame, Kenneth (1859–1932), writer and novelist, best remembered for his children's classic, *The Wind in the Willows*.

Greville, Charles (1794–1865), politician, for many years clerk to the Privy Council. A trusted confidant of Whigs and Tories, he kept a detailed personal and political journal for forty years.

Haggard, Sir H. Rider (1856–1925), novelist, notably the author of *She* and *King Solomon's Mines*.

Hardy, Emma (1840–1912), first wife of Thomas Hardy. The marriage was far from happy, but on Emma's death Hardy seemed to undergo a somewhat belated change of heart and wrote some of his best and most moving poetry in memory of her.

Hardy, Thomas (1840–1928), novelist, poet and dramatist.

Hartley, Dorothy (1893–1985), writer, she trained as an art teacher before becoming an historian of English life.

Harton, F.P., the vicar of Baulking, in Oxfordshire.

Hawker, Colonel Peter (1786–1853), captain of the 14th Light Dragoons during the Peninsular War, he retired from the Army in 1813. Became Lieutenant-Colonel of the North Hampshire Militia.

Hawkes, Jacquetta (b.1910), archaeologist and writer, married to J.B. Priestley.

Herbert, George (1593–1633), poet and clergyman.

Hind, Penelope (1759–1846), kept a detailed journal from 1787 to 1838; she married William Banwell in 1796 after an eight-year engagement, only to be widowed when he died of typhus three months after the wedding. She was to be a widow for twelve years, then became the wife of John Hind, vicar of Findon in Sussex.

Hodgson, Ralph (1871–1962), poet, artist and, briefly, a publisher, he left England in 1924 to live in Japan, until 1938 when he moved to America, remaining there until his death.

Hodson, David (b.1920), land agent, poet and hurdle maker.

Hogg, James (1770–1835), poet. Discovered by Sir Walter Scott, to whom he sent his poems whilst still a shepherd, he became known as the 'Ettrick Shepherd' and was a friend of Byron, Wordsworth and other literary figures.

Hopkins, Gerard Manley (1844–89), poet, classical scholar and Jesuit priest.

Housman, A.E. (1859–1936), classicist and poet.

Hughes, Anne (late 18th C), a farmer's wife, living near Chepstow, she kept a journal of daily events for one year only, from 1796 to 1797.

Hughes, Richard (1900–76), dramatist, novelist and writer.

Huxley, Elspeth (b.1907), novelist, biographer and travel writer, she is perhaps best-known for her famous book, *The Flame Trees of Thika*.

James I and VI (1566–1625), king of Scotland at nine months old, he succeeded Elizabeth I to the English throne in 1603.

Jonson, Ben (1572–1637), dramatist, poet, scholar and writer of court masques.

Kilvert, Revd Francis (1840–79), curate at Langley Burrell, Clyro, and at St Harmon's; becoming vicar of Bredwardine in 1877.

Kipling, Rudyard (1865–1936), poet, novelist and short-story writer. He won the Nobel Prize for Literature in 1907, the first English writer to do so.

Lane, Margaret, novelist and biographer, notably of the Brontës and Beatrix Potter.

Larkin, Philip (1922–85), poet.

Lee, Laurie (b.1914), poet and writer.

Lodge, Thomas (1558–1625), writer and poet, best remembered for his romance, *Rosalynde*.

Macaulay, Rose (1881–1958), novelist, essayist and travel writer.

Marlowe, Christopher (1564–93), poet and dramatist.

Masefield, John (1878–1967), poet and novelist, became poet laureate in 1930.

Mew, Charlotte (1869–1928), poet and short-story writer. She was driven to suicide by family and financial problems.

Milne, A.A. (1882–1956), dramatist, poet and novelist, best remembered for his children's books.

Milton, John (1608–74), poet.

Mitford, Nancy (1904–73), writer and biographer. The senior scribe of the indefatigable Mitford family.

Morris, Dr Claver (1659–1727), physician in Wells, he married three times.

Morris, William (1834–96), poet, novelist and painter, member of the Pre-Raphaelite Brotherhood and founding father of the Arts and Crafts movement.

Moseley, Sydney (1888–1961), journalist and writer.

Muggeridge, Malcolm (1903–90), writer and television personality, he was editor of *Punch* from 1953 to 1957.

Nash, Thomas (1567–1601), writer, satirist and opponent of Puritanism.

Newton, Revd Benjamin (1761–1830), held various livings in Wiltshire, Somerset and Yorkshire. Became chaplain to the Duke of Portland and magistrate for the North Riding of Yorkshire.

Partridge, Frances (b.1900), writer and translator, after taking her degree at Newnham College, Cambridge, she worked for a time at David Garnett's and Francis Birrell's London bookshop, which was a centre for the Bloomsbury Group. In 1933 she married Ralph Partridge, a friend of Lytton Strachey.

Pearson, Hesketh (1887–1964), actor and biographer.

Pitter, Ruth (b.1897), poet, her first poem was published when she was thirteen in the socialist weekly, *New Age*. In 1955 she was the first woman to receive the Queen's Gold Medal for Poetry.

Pope, Alexander (1688–1744), poet and satirist.

Powys, T.F. (1875–1953), writer and novelist, much of his work is set against the West Country background in which he lived.

Raverat, Gwen (1885–1957), wood engraver and writer, she was the grand-daughter of Charles Darwin. She illustrated a number of works, including several anthologies in association with Kenneth Grahame.

Rossetti, Christina (1830–94), poet. The sister of Dante Gabriel Rossetti, she shared her brother's intellectual interests and many of his friends, despite being forced to live quietly at home through severe ill-health.

Rossetti, Dante Gabriel (1828–82), pre-Raphaelite painter and poet.

Sassoon, Siegfried (1886–1967), writer and poet, best remembered for the poetry he wrote in the trenches during the First World War.

Sekers, Simone, food writer and journalist.

Shakespeare, William (1564–1616), playwright and poet.

Shelley, Percy Bysshe (1792–1822), poet.

Sidney, Sir Robert (1563–1626), created Baron Sidney by James I in 1603, Viscount Lisle in 1605, and Earl of Leicester in 1618.

Skinner, Revd John (1772–*c*.1839), parish priest of Camerton, Somerset from 1800.

Smith, Revd Sydney (1771–1845), Canon of St Paul's from 1831 and the author of numerous letters, reviews and essays.

Temple, Revd J.W. (1739–96), rector of Mamhead, Exeter.

Thomas, Dylan (1914–53), poet.

Thomas, Edward (1878–1917), poet and writer, he turned to poetry after meeting Robert Frost in 1913, but the majority of his poetry was unpublished until after he was killed at Arras in 1917.

Thomas, R.S. (b.1913), poet and clergyman. Until his retirement in 1978 he was vicar of St Hywyn, Aberdaron with Y Rhiw and Llanfaelrhys.

Thomson, James (1700–48), poet. The son of a Scottish minister, Thomson is perhaps best known for 'The Seasons', one of English literature's most popular poems.

Treneer, Anne (1891–1966), writer and biographer, she was born and bred in Cornwall.

Turner, Thomas (1729–93), Sussex schoolmaster, he gave up teaching to open a general store.

Tusser, Thomas (1524–80), agricultural poet and writer.

Walpole, Horace (1717–97), fourth Earl of Orford, poet, essayist and novelist, Walpole was an enthusiast of the Gothic, creating 'a little Gothic castle' at his house in Twickenham, Strawberry Hill.

Warner, Sylvia Townsend (1893–1978), poet and novelist.

Welch, Denton (1915–48), novelist and diarist, when he was twenty he was knocked off his bicycle by a car, suffering appalling injuries, as a result of which he died thirteen years later.

White, Gilbert (1720–93), naturalist and writer, he was the curate of Selborne, where he was born, for most of his life.

Witts, Revd Francis (1783–1854), rector of Upper Slaughter, Gloucestershire, and later vicar of Stanway.

Woodforde, Revd James (1740–1803), sub-warden of New College, Oxford, until 1774 when he became rector of Weston Longeville, Norfolk. Remembered for his diary, *The Diary of a Country Parson*, which was published in five volumes.

Woolf, Virginia (1882–1941), writer and novelist, she became a key member of the Bloomsbury Group.

Wordsworth, Dorothy (1771–1855), sister of William Wordsworth.

Wordsworth, William (1770–1850), poet.

Young, Andrew (1885–1971), poet, critic and naturalist.

ACKNOWLEDGEMENTS

The author and publishers gratefully acknowledge permission to reprint the following material:

'Wiltshire Downs' by Andrew Young, reproduced by kind permission of The Andrew Young Estate; extract from *London and the Life of Literature in Late Victorian England: The Diary of George Gissing*, ed. George Coustillas, reproduced by kind permission of The Harvester Press; extract from *Prospect of Britain* by Jacquetta Hawkes, reproduced by kind permission of HarperCollins Publishers Ltd; extract from Ruth Pitter's 'Dun-Colour' is reproduced from *Collected Poems* (Enitharmon Press, 1990); extracts from *Cider with Rosie* by Laurie Lee, reproduced by kind permission of The Hogarth Press; extracts from *Kilvert's Diaries*, ed. William Plomer, reproduced by kind permission of the estate of William Plomer and Jonathan Cape; extract from *The Tale of Beatrix Potter* by Margaret Lane, © Frederick Warne & Co., 1968, reproduced by permission of Frederick Warne & Co.; extract from *The Diary of a Cotswold Parson (Rev Francis Witts)*, ed. David Verey, reproduced by kind permission of Alan Sutton Publishing; extracts from *Gallipot Eyes* by Elspeth Huxley, reproduced by kind permission of Hutchinson; extract from *Everything to Lose* by Frances Partridge, copyright © 1985 Frances Partridge, printed by permission of Rogers, Coleridge & White Ltd; extract from *The Diary of Virginia Woolf*, ed. Anne Olivier Bell, reproduced by kind permission of the Estate of Virginia Woolf and The Hogarth Press; 'Long Lion Days' by Philip Larkin, from *Collected Poems* by Philip Larkin, ed. Anthony Thwaite, reproduced by kind permission of Faber and Faber Ltd; extract from *Summoned by Bells* by John Betjeman, reproduced by kind permission of John Murray (Publishers) Ltd; extract from *Period Piece* by Gwen Raverat, reproduced by kind permission of Faber and Faber Ltd; extract from *Another Part of the Wood* by Kenneth Clarke reproduced by kind permission of John Murray (Publishers) Ltd; 'Up on the Downs' by John Masefield, reproduced by kind permission of the Society of Authors as the literary representative of the Estate of John Masefield; extract from 'The Burning of the Leaves' by

Laurence Binyon, reproduced by kind permission of Mrs Nicolete Gray and the Society of Authors on behalf of the Laurence Binyon Estate; extract from *Siegfried Sassoon's Diaries*, ed. Rupert Hart-Davis, reproduced by kind permission of Faber and Faber Ltd; extracts from *A Suffolk Childhood* by Simon Dewes, reproduced by kind permission of Hutchinson; extract from *The Peregrine* by J.A. Baker, reproduced by kind permission of Collins, an imprint of HarperCollins Publishers Limited; extracts from *Collected Letters of Sylvia Townsend Warner*, ed. William Maxwell, reproduced by kind permission of the Estate of Sylvia Townsend Warner, William Maxwell and Chatto & Windus; extract from *Diary of a Farmer's Wife* by Anne Hughes (Allen Lane, 1980), copyright © Mollie Preston, reproduced by permission of Penguin Books Ltd; extract from *The Diaries of Malcolm Muggeridge*, ed. John Bright-Homes (HarperCollins), reproduced by kind permission of David Higham Associates; extract from *Made in England* by Dorothy Hartley, © Dorothy Hartley 1939, reproduced by kind permission of Sheil Land Associates; extract from *The House at Pooh Corner* by A.A. Milne, © 1956 A.A. Milne, reproduced by kind permission of Methuen Children's Books; 'Thaw' by Philip Larkin, from *Collected Poems* by Philip Larkin, ed. Anthony Thwaite, reproduced by kind permission of Faber and Faber Ltd; 'Graveyard in Norfolk' from *Selected Poems* (1985) by Sylvia Townsend Warner, ed. Claire Harman, reproduced by kind permission of Carcanet Press Ltd; extract from 'A Dumb Animal' from *Rosie Plum and Other Stories* by T.F. Powys, reproduced by kind permission of Chatto & Windus Ltd; 'Eve' by Ralph Hodgson, reproduced by kind permission of Macmillan London Ltd; extract from *The Towers of Trebizond* by Rose Macaulay, reproduced by kind permission of HarperCollins Publishers Ltd; extract from *The Smith of Smiths* by Hesketh Pearson, reproduced by kind permission of A.P. Watt on behalf of Michael Holroyd; extract from *Memories of Christmas* by Dylan Thomas, reproduced by kind permission of J.M. Dent & Sons; extract from *Armstrong's Norfolk Diary*, ed. Herbert B.J. Armstrong, reproduced by kind permission of Hodder & Stoughton Ltd/New English Library Ltd; extract from *Essex Schooldays* by Simon Dewes, reproduced by kind permission of Hutchinson.

The publishers have made every effort to trace copyright ownership and would be grateful to learn of any unwitting copyright infringement.

LIST OF ILLUSTRATIONS

29 Bruton Street, London W1/The Bridgeman Art Library.

Page 77: Gathering lupins near Chichester, *c.* 1930. Popperfoto.

Pages 80/81: Harvesters taking a break in the Thames Valley, pre-war. Rural History Centre, University of Reading.

Pages 84/5: *Midsummer Evening* by James Hayllar, 1867. Fine Art Photographic.

Page 91: Mother and child, 1833. The Mansell Collection.

Pages 96/7: Children on a wall, Ditchear, 1933. Rural History Centre, University of Reading.

Pages 100/101: *Jack O' Lantern* by Arthur Hughes. Christies, London/Bridgeman Art Library.

Page 105: Swimming a witch, from *Witches Apprehended, Examined and Executed*, 1613. Fortean Picture Library.

Pages 108/109: The Horn Dance at Abbott's Bromley, Staffs, 1933. Hulton Deutsch Collection.

Pages 112/13: *An English Autumn Afternoon* by Ford Maddox Brown. By permission of the Birmingham Museum and Art Gallery.

Page 116: The celebration of the Harvest Home, *c.* 1770. E.T. Archive.

Page 118: Harvesting a wartime onion crop in Kent. Rural History Centre, University of Reading.

Pages 120/1: *A Country Cricket Match* by John Reid, 1878. Tate Gallery, London.

Page 125: Shooting Flying, from *The Gentleman's Recreation* by Richard Blome, 1686.

Page 129: The rabbit trapper, 1948. Rural History Centre, University of Reading.

Pages 132/3: *The Cottage Home* by William H. Snape. Christopher Wood Gallery, London/The Bridgeman Art Library.

Page 137: Scene from an angora rabbit farm, Gloucestershire, 1935. Rural History Centre, University of Reading.

Page 142: Illustration by E.H. Shepard from *The Wind in the Willows* by Kenneth Grahame, copyright under the Berne Convention, reproduced by permission of Curtis Brown, London. For Canada and the US: reprinted with the permission of Charles Scribner's Sons, an imprint of Macmillan Publishing Company, from *The Wind in the Willows* by Kenneth Grahame, illustrated by Ernest H. Shepard. Copyright 1933, 1953, 1954 Charles Scribner's Sons; copyright renewed © 1961 Ernest H. Shepard.

Pages 148/9: *Man with a Jug* by Charles Spencelayh. Private Collection, England. Courtesy Sotheby's.

Page 157: Gipsy family with traditional horse-drawn bow-top van. Rural History Centre, University of Reading.

Pages 160/61: *Wild Garden, Winter* by John Nash, 1959. Tate Gallery, London. Courtesy the Trustees of the John Nash Estate.

Page 164: Farm chores, December, from a fifteenth-century Book of Hours. Add. 24098.f.29V. By permission of the British Library, London.

Page 167: Harvesting a crop of January potatoes, 1956. Rural History Centre, University of Reading.

Pages 168/9: *All Saints Church, Hastings* by David Cox, 1812. Birmingham City Museums & Art Gallery/Bridgeman Art Library.

Page 172: *Church Interior* by W.H. Hunt. Private Collection, England. Courtesy Sotheby's.

Page 182: The Bishop of Oxford, 1902. Rural History Centre, University of Reading.

Pages 184/5: *Fête in Petworth Park* by W.F. Witherington, 1835. National Trust Photo Library/Derrick E. Witty.

Page 190: *Farmer Giles and his wife shewing off their daughter Betty* by James Gillray, 1809. The Mansell Collection.

Pages 194/5: A family picnic at Sulham House, *c.* 1889. Rural History Centre, University of Reading. Courtesy Mrs I. Moon.

Pages 200/201: *The Christmas Tree* by A. Chevallier Taylor. Private Collection/ Bridgeman Art Library.

Page 204: Children carol singing from *Book of Days* by R. Chambers. Rural History Centre, University of Reading.

Page 210–11: Wassailing the apple trees, Somerset, on Twelfth Night, 1931. Hulton Deutsch Collection.

INDEX